To Nathan,
with best wishes

David B

LAWLESS

LAWLESS

The Obama Administration's
Unprecedented Assault on the
Constitution and the Rule of Law

DAVID E. BERNSTEIN

Encounter Books
New York • London

First American edition published in 2015 by Encounter Books, an activity of Encounter for Culture and Education, Inc., a nonprofit, tax exempt corporation.
Encounter Books website address: www.encounterbooks.com

Manufactured in the United States and printed on acid-free paper. The paper used in this publication meets the minimum requirements of ANSI/NISO Z39.48–1992 (R 1997) (*Permanence of Paper*).

FIRST AMERICAN EDITION

LIBRARY OF CONGRESS CATALOGING-IN-PUBLICATION DATA
Bernstein, David E., author.
Lawless : the Obama administration's unprecedented assault on the Constitution and the rule of law / David E. Bernstein.
pages   cm
Includes bibliographical references and index.
ISBN 978-1-59403-833-4 (hardback) — ISBN 978-1-59403-834-1 (ebook)
1. Constitutional history—United States—21st century.   2. Rule of law—United States.   3. Executive power—United States.   4. United States—Politics and government—2009–   5. Obama, Barack.   I. Title.
KF4541.B447 2015
342.7302'9—dc23
2015017132

PRODUCED BY WILSTED & TAYLOR PUBLISHING SERVICES
Copy editor Jennifer Brown
Design and composition Nancy Koerner
Indexer Derek Gottlieb

CONTENTS

FOREWORD

Senator Ted Cruz

When Barack Obama first ran for president, many of his supporters, including much of the media, portrayed him as a near-messianic figure who had the potential to heal old wounds, purify our politics, and bring together a divided nation. Columnist Ezra Klein, for example, wrote (in a not-so-subtle Christological allusion) that Obama was "not the Word made flesh, but the triumph of word *over* flesh, over color, over despair."[1] *San Francisco Chronicle* columnist Mark Morford agreed with his "spiritually advanced" friends who "identif[ied] Obama as a Lightworker, that rare kind of attuned being . . . who can actually help usher in *a new way of being on the planet.*" Obama, Morford wrote, was like a "philosopher[ ] and peacemaker[ ] of a very high order," a person who speaks "not just to reason or emotion, but to the soul."[2] Not to be outdone, Obama's wife, Michelle, told campaign audiences that her husband was the one candidate who understood that "before we can work on the [nation's] problems, we have to fix our souls." "I am married to the only person in this race," said Michelle Obama, "who has a chance of healing this nation."[3] To top things off, *Time* magazine's post-election cover story about the new president began this way: "Some princes are born in palaces.

Some are born in mangers. But a few are born in the imagination, out of scraps of history and hope."[4]

Rather than temper the absurdly high expectations others were setting for him, Obama often doubled down by promising to usher in a higher form of politics—a statesmanship that would transcend our petty ideological divisions and cynical partisanship. While announcing his candidacy, for instance, Obama explained that he was not in the race "just to hold an office, but to gather with you to transform a nation" and to "usher in a new birth of freedom on this Earth."[5] Along these same lines, he promised to "not allow us to be distracted by the same politics that seeks to divide us with false charges and meaningless labels."[6] He not only vowed "to fundamentally change how Washington works,"[7] but he also declared that he would "fundamentally transform[ ]" the entire United States.[8] When he won the Democratic nomination, he grandiosely declared that "generations from now, we will be able to look back and tell our children that . . . this was the moment when the rise of the oceans began to slow and our planet began to heal."[9] And in his first inaugural address, Obama proclaimed "an end to the petty grievances and false promises, the recriminations and worn-out dogmas that for far too long have strangled our politics."[10]

Looking back on these extravagant claims, one cannot escape the sense that a fraud has been perpetrated on the American people. President Obama *has* transformed America—but not in the way he advertised. With the enactment of "Obamacare," he transformed the nation's healthcare system (for the worse). With the passage of Dodd-Frank, he transformed the nation's financial regulatory regime (for the worse). And by appeasing Cuba and Iran—the latter openly calling for "Death to America" and "Death to Israel"—he transformed the nation's foreign policy (for the worse). But in the midst of these transformations, it became abundantly clear that Obama never had any intention of transcending ideology, bridging the partisan divide, and elevating our discourse. In many ways, he has made our politics even more corrosive. Instead of "fundamentally chang[ing] how Washington works," the president has been all too willing to engage in outright deceit, rank partisanship, cronyism, and procedural gimmickry to enact his agenda.

Obamacare is the perfect example. There's no question that Obamacare was built on outright deceit. As the bill worked its way through the legislative process, the president traveled the country trying to sell it to the American people. Most infamously, he promised over and over again, "If you like your health care plan, you can keep it."[11] This claim, necessary to curry what little public support the bill was able to achieve, was a blatant falsehood. As for bipartisanship, the president could not garner a single Republican vote for his sweeping and constitutionally flawed healthcare proposal. But instead of enacting a more modest reform that could earn bipartisan support, he pressed forward, taunting Republicans all along the way. ("The election's over," he once chided Senator John McCain in response to McCain's protests about the clandestine nature of the bill's development.[12]) And how about cronyism? To get the Democratic votes he needed, the president had to cut shady deals with vacillating senators—who can forget the "Cornhusker Kickback" and "Louisiana Purchase"—and bestow favors on labor unions, the insurance industry, and other special interests. Then the improbable happened: Democratic Senator Ted Kennedy passed away and was replaced by Republican Scott Brown. As a result, the president lost his filibuster-proof majority in the Senate. Which leads us, finally, to procedural gimmickry. No longer able to pass a House-Senate compromise bill, the president instead rammed through the Senate version that had originally passed with Kennedy's vote by abusing a legislative procedure known as "reconciliation."[13] Hardly the product of a "new politics" that Obama had promised, the president's signature legislative achievement stands instead as a testament to all that is rotten about Washington.

Time and again, under the banner of high-sounding ideals, President Obama acts in a way completely counter to those ideals. Not only do his actions fail to match his words, but they often track in the opposite direction. This Orwellian habit is starkly displayed in the Obama administration's approach to governmental openness and transparency. Shortly after assuming the presidency, President Obama issued a memo committing his administration "to creating an unprecedented level of openness in government."[14] In a speech that same day, the president declared that "there's been too much secrecy in this city," and he assured the nation that "[t]hat era is now over."[15] He has even gone so far as to claim that his administration "is the most transparent administration in history."[16] Nothing could be further from the truth. Soon after Obama publicly praised the Freedom of Information Act (FOIA) and committed his administration "not simply to live up to the letter but also the spirit of this law,"[17] his White House counsel secretly instructed executive branch departments and agencies to submit—to the White House—*all* outside document requests that involved "White House equities."[18] This unprecedented move allowed the president to filter politically sensitive information, which of course prolonged the release of any such information to the press and public in violation of FOIA disclosure deadlines.[19] Needless to say, such a maneuver is *not* in the spirit of FOIA, nor is it remotely in line with Obama's verbal paeans to transparency.

Sadly, this is just the tip of the iceberg. Abusive and covert behavior has proven to be the rule, rather than the exception, in this administration. But don't take it from me. Listen to some of the president's most lavish supporters—the media. According to the *San Francisco Chronicle*, the president "had a decidedly fraught relationship with media scrutiny" from the beginning of his *first* term.[20] It would only go downhill from there. By the end of four years, one *Atlantic* writer had seen enough:

> Obama's first term has in fact been rife with just the sort of opacity that breeds corruption, obscures misdeeds, and undermines public trust in government. Far from being praiseworthy, the prevailing executive-branch attitude toward secrecy is an abomination, as is evident from even a cursory look at its real-world manifestations. . . . Contrary to its claims, the Obama Administration just may be the least transparent in American history.[21]

The situation did not improve after the president's reelection. Over halfway through Obama's second term, a *Washington Post* blog documented how this administration has (1) fought court battles to avoid disclosing White House visitors; (2) "simply ignor[ed]" the federal open meetings law; (3) withheld secret legal memos, including one saying the CIA could kill US citizens affiliated with terrorists; (4) "aggressively" utilized the "state secrets privilege"; and (5) uncompromisingly attacked whistleblowers and "prosecuted more leakers under the Espionage Act *than all other administrations combined.*"[22] So much for President Obama's promise of "unprecedented openness" and "transparency."

So what does any of this have to do with Professor David Bernstein's excellent book? Well, as bad as the foregoing bait and switches are, they pale in comparison to the Obama administration's lawlessness. Rather than remain within constitutional boundaries, President Obama has defiantly flouted them. More so than any other administration in our country's history, his has trampled roughshod over our defining ideal, the rule of law. And he has done so in exactly the same way as was done in the previous examples: essentially promising the moon, only to confiscate the citizenry's moon pies. On his first day in office, Obama assured the public that the rule of law would be a "touchstone[ ] of this presidency."[23] But this promise has proven every bit as illusory as the other promises he has made.

President Obama rarely lets the law stand in the way of his designs—almost always putting ideology above fidelity to the law. As a consequence, the list of his usurpations runs long.[24] In an ironic turn, for example, the Obama administration has blatantly violated Obamacare's clear statutory text on numerous occasions to avoid the political consequences of actually enforcing the law. This was Obama's signature piece of legislation, and yet even *he* refused to abide by its legal requirements. The Obama administration has also refused to faithfully enforce the nation's immigration laws. Even though Congress had repeatedly rejected legislation that would offer amnesty to certain children of illegal immigrants who were illegally brought to the United States at a young age, Obama nevertheless implemented parts of this DREAM Act by executive fiat. A couple of years later, the president went even further, attempting to extend lawful presence and work authorization—essentially counterfeiting immigration papers contrary to federal statute—to nearly five million more illegal immigrants. He did all of this without a shred of legal authority.[25]

There are countless other, lesser known, but equally pernicious, usurpations. The Obama Justice Department, for instance, categorically refuses to prosecute certain drug offenses because the administration disagrees with the sentences that the law requires. The Obama administration has essentially gutted President Clinton's 1996 welfare reform law by waiving—again, without legal authority—the work requirements that are the centerpiece of the law.[26] And on a matter closer to home for me, the president defied the Constitution by making numerous "recess" appointments to the National Labor Relations Board, even though the Senate was not in recess. So egregious was the president's power grab that even the Supreme Court *unanimously* held that the president had violated the Constitution.[27] These examples barely scratch the surface of Obama's lawlessness, as Professor Bernstein exhaustively details in his book.

But none of this should have been all that surprising. President Obama and the officials who populate his administration are self-styled progressives, and American progressives have long viewed the Constitution as something to be overcome, not something to be followed faithfully. To progressives, the "separation of powers" and "checks and balances"—concepts designed to protect the natural rights of the people—are hopelessly outmoded ideas that impede the ability of "enlightened" government elites to fix modern problems. As Professor Ronald Pestritto of Hillsdale College puts it, the first progressives "sought to enlarge vastly the scope of the national government for the purpose of responding to a set of economic and social conditions that, it was contended, could not have been envisioned during the founding era, and for which the Founders' limited, constitutional government was inadequate."[28] They, therefore, "took aim both at the Constitution, where the separation of powers inhibited the kind of activist central government that would be essential to implementing the Progressive policy agenda, and at the Declaration of Independence," with its embrace of natural rights, "which the Progressives rightly understood as setting the purpose for the Constitution itself."[29]

Woodrow Wilson, who was one of the earliest theoreticians and practitioners of progressive politics, voiced all of these themes. Of the Constitution, Wilson wrote that it "is not honored by blind worship" and that a "fearless criticism" of our constitutional system was the first step necessary for "emancipation" from that system.[30] For Wilson, self-government should be a "straightforward thing of simple method, single, *unstinted* power, and clear responsibility."[31] Checks and balances were detrimental to that end: "No living thing can have its organs offset against each other as checks, and live," he wrote.[32] "Government," according to Wilson, "is not a machine, but a living thing," and "[i]t is modified by its environment, necessitated by its tasks, shaped to its functions by the sheer pressure of life."[33] "Living political constitutions," in short, "must be Darwinian in structure and in practice," not Newtonian, as the framers had designed the United States Constitution to be.[34] With this, Wilson planted the seeds of "living constitutionalism"—the concept that the Constitution's meaning is not fixed but should be adapted to the changing circumstances of the times.[35]

Wilson's notion of a "living Constitution" is wholeheartedly embraced by modern progressives—and President Obama is no exception. In his campaign polemic *The Audacity of Hope*, then–Senator Obama wrote that the Constitution "is not a static but rather a living document, and must be read in the context of an ever-changing world."[36] And as president, he declared that "we have always understood that when times change, so must we; that fidelity to our founding principles requires new responses to new challenges."[37] Certainly, as Professor Bernstein notes in his book, Obama has occasionally expressed admiration for the Constitution and its separation of powers, as any national politician must. But in a 2001 radio interview, while he was still a state senator in Illinois, Obama voiced disappointment that the Constitution has been interpreted only as "a charter of negative liberties" and not also as a charter of positive rights that spells out what government "must do on your behalf." He complained that the Supreme Court under Chief Justice Earl Warren—a Court that often *abandoned* strict adherence to the text, history, and structure of the Constitution—did not go far enough, because it "never ventured into the issues of redistribution of wealth" and "more basic issues of political and economic justice in this society." According to Obama, the Warren Court failed to "break free from the essential constraints that were placed by the Founding

Fathers in the Constitution."[38] Like Wilson, Obama clearly distrusts even the most fundamental aspects of the framers' handiwork. Instead, he suggests that courts should contort the Constitution to mandate vast redistributions of wealth.

But even more importantly, Obama's actions have spoken far louder than his words. What was expressed back then as mere disappointment with our constitutional design and history eventually became an all-out revolt against the Constitution, especially after Democrats lost control of Congress midway through President Obama's first term. No longer able to enact his agenda through Congress, and unwilling to compromise, Obama began to take matters into his own hands by claiming he had the power to act when Congress would not, as though his powers were somehow enlarged the moment Congress refused to address his priorities. Veteran unemployment? "We can't simply wait for Congress to do its job. . . . If Congress won't act, I will."[39] Food and Drug Administration reform? "[W]e can't wait for action on the Hill."[40] Climate change? "But if Congress won't act soon to protect future generations, I will."[41] The economy? "But where Congress won't act, I will."[42] Immigration? Where Obama himself used to declare that he had no authority to act—"I am not king," he memorably observed[43]—Obama now declares: "[T]he American people don't want me just standing around twiddling my thumbs and waiting for Congress to get something done."[44] And on and on and on.

President Obama has inverted our constitutional system of government. Article I of the Constitution gives Congress sole power to make laws, and Article II tasks the president with *executing the laws that Congress has made.* The president has no more authority to do Congress's job (i.e., make laws) when it won't act than a senator has to do the *president's* job when he won't act in the way we would prefer (which is often the case with this president). This separation of powers is foundational to our system of government precisely because it helps ensure liberty for all Americans. As James Madison wrote in *Federalist* No. 47, the concentration of executive, legislative, and judicial power "in the same hands" is "the very definition of tyranny." So long as Madison's maxim holds true, the separation of powers should *never* be discarded for ideological objectives, much less for political convenience.

Although he would never say so, President Obama's actions suggest that he does not believe (or just does not care) in the truth Madison described. According to Obama, congressional inaction is not—and should not be—a limitation on his power to act. If anything, he sees it as a license to act. President Obama's repeated threats to take action because of Congress's inability or unwillingness to do so, unfortunately, bear an uncanny resemblance to Julius Caesar's response to political gridlock. The demise of the Roman republic and the emergence of Caesar's dictatorship were partly the result of Caesar's frustration with the logjam known as the Roman political system. According to classicist Anthony Everitt, Caesar thought the solution to the problems of the Roman constitution "with its endless checks and balances" was "a completely new system of government," one that made him all-powerful.[45]

Of course, no one seriously believes that President Obama aspires to be caesar. When his term ends, he will step aside as every president in our history has done. But President Obama's raw assertions of power will undermine, if not transform, our constitutional order if they are not repudiated. Future presidents now have mountains of lawless precedent to call upon, should they desire to enact their own wishes contra the preferences of the American people as represented by Congress and expressed in their laws. Law professor Jonathan Turley, himself a liberal, has drawn largely the same conclusion: "We are seeing the emergence of a different model of government in our country—a model long ago rejected by the Framers."[46] "What's emerging," he says, "is an imperial presidency, an über-presidency . . . where the President can act unilaterally."[47] As Professor Turley witheringly observed, "the painful fact is that Barack Obama is the president that Nixon always wanted to be."[48] This should greatly alarm anyone who still believes in limited, republican government and the rule of law—even those who happen to agree with the substance of President Obama's policies.

And this brings us back to Professor Bernstein's book. As Obama's presidency comes to an end, it is important that the historical record be clear about the lawlessness that has transpired. That is what Professor Bernstein's book does, and for that, he has done the nation a great service. He chronicles in fair, but excruciating, detail the many ways the Obama administration has subverted the rule of law—the politicization of the Justice Department; the disregard of Congress in foreign affairs; the assault on property rights; the use of unaccountable "czars" to circumvent the Senate confirmation process; the targeting of politically disfavored individuals and groups (including by the IRS); and the attacks on free exercise of religion, freedom of speech, and due process of law, among numerous other injustices. Although many have openly *cheered* the president's actions, while others have downplayed or ignored their significance, Professor Bernstein makes a compelling case for why those actions should be viewed for what they are: an unprecedented assault on the Constitution and the rule of law. And it is a case that future historians should not, and will not be able to, ignore. Subversion of the law is President Obama's true legacy, and it is a legacy that could have a lasting and devastating impact on the future of our country if we let it. The only question now is: Will we?

INTRODUCTION

President Barack Obama has presided over one constitutional debacle after another. Given the potentially permanent damage the Obama administration has done and continues to do to the Constitution and the rule of law, and the bad precedents that have been set for future administrations, someone needed to step up and document how and why the Obama administration has been undermining our constitutional system. So to paraphrase the great Rabbi Hillel, if not me, who, and if not now, when?

It wasn't supposed to be this way. Obama ran for president in 2008 as a candidate who would respect the Constitution and restore the rule of law after years of perceived neglect. He told one audience, "I taught the Constitution for ten years, I believe in the Constitution, and I will obey the Constitution of the United States."[1] At another campaign appearance, he promised to adhere to the Constitution and the rule of law. "The separation of powers works. Our Constitution works," he told the crowd.[2]

Respecting the separation of powers—the constitutional division of power among the president's executive branch, Congress, and the courts—was a theme candidate Obama returned to again and again. "The biggest problems that we're facing right now," he explained, "have to do with George Bush trying to bring more and more power into the executive branch and not go through Congress at all. And that's what I intend to reverse when I'm president."[3]

Many voters were sure they could rely on Obama to fulfill these promises. Obama seemed to embody a thread in the tradition of American legal liberalism that respects civil liberties and the legal process, and tries to limit the president's power to undertake mischief behind Congress's back. Plus, Obama used to teach constitutional law at the University of Chicago, reinforcing the perception that he respected the Constitution. Even many conservative lawyers believed that Obama would take his constitutional responsibilities seriously and respect the rule of law.

My liberal constitutional law professor colleagues, meanwhile, were positively giddy at the prospect of an Obama presidency. George Washington University professor Jeffrey Rosen predicted in early 2008 that if Barack Obama were to become president, "he would be, among other things, our first civil libertarian president."[4] Rosen even worried that an Obama administration might become paralyzed by Obama's fear that taking bold but necessary actions might violate the Constitution.[5]

Enthusiasm among liberal civil libertarians only grew when Obama won the election. On Inauguration Day in January 2009, lawyers representing terrorism suspects being held as prisoners of war without trial, a product of one of George W. Bush's most controversial exercises of presidential power, "formed a boisterous conga line." Their expectations of Obama were clear: "Rule of law, baby!" they chanted.[6]

To borrow a phrase from Wall Street, up on rumor, down on fact. There has never been a greater gap between a presidential candidate's constitutional promises and his actions in the Oval Office. Instead of rolling back presidential power, President Obama has often bragged about ignoring Congress and pursuing actions of questionable legality on his own because Congress refused to rubber-stamp his initiatives.

Obama's defense of these actions has not been some well-developed-but-debatable theory of presidential power. Rather, Obama has consistently relied on the mere assertion that "we can't wait" for Congress to legislate the way he wants it to. For example, Obama told a Las Vegas audience in October 2011, "We can't wait for an increasingly dysfunctional Congress to do its job. Where they won't act, I will."[7] In July 2013, he expanded the genre, exclaiming that not just the American people, but the world "can't wait for Congress to get its act together."[8]

In February 2014, Obama promised that "wherever I can take steps to expand opportunity, to help working families, that's what I'm going to do with or without Congress. I want to work with them, but I can't wait for them."[9] Later that year, when Republicans in Congress began strategizing about how to challenge Obama's illegal actions in court, Obama proclaimed, "Middle-class families can't wait for Republicans in Congress to do stuff." This sort of rhetoric became so common that the president began referring to his "We Can't Wait announcements."[10]

And it wasn't mere rhetorical flourish. Consider some of President Obama's initiatives that bypass Congress, exactly what candidate Obama swore not to do. Among other things, President Obama

- has delayed, modified, and ignored various provisions of the Affordable Care Act ("Obamacare") with barely a pretense of the legal authority to do so;

- first launched military action in Libya without congressional approval and then violated the War Powers Resolution, with the absurd rationale that bombing Libya was not "hostilities" under the law;

- used his recess appointments power when the Senate was not, in fact, in recess, as the Constitution requires;

- granted indefinite amnesty and work permits to hundreds of thousands of illegal aliens;

- violated and undermined federal bankruptcy law to benefit the autoworkers' union and to the detriment of bondholders who had priority under the law;

- appointed high-level "czars" to evade the Constitution's requirement that high-level government officials receive Senate approval; and

- ignored a law requiring him to give thirty days notice to Congress before releasing prisoners from confinement in Guantanamo Bay, Cuba.

These actions led to charges that, consistent with his own 2008 campaign rhetoric, by circumventing Congress President Obama was acting unconstitutionally. When asked about these accusations, he simply taunted his critics, "So sue me!"[11]

Meanwhile, the president has allowed his underlings to run amok constitutionally. Obama appointees have

- tried to impose an unconstitutional nationwide speech code on college campuses;

- argued to the Supreme Court that the First Amendment's guarantee of freedom of religion does not protect churches' right to choose their clergy;

- shown such extreme contempt for the rights of property owners that the Obama administration lost several property rights cases 9–0 in the Supreme Court;

- tried to force public schools nationwide to use racial quotas in determining how and when to punish students for misbehaving; and

- forced universities nationwide to strip college students accused of sexual misconduct of long-standing procedural protections meant to ensure fairness.

Perhaps worst of all, the Justice Department, charged with enforcing the nation's laws, and already politicized and partisan under previous administrations, has become even more so.

The Obama administration has also been egregiously indifferent to freedom of speech. As of this writing, we have no direct evidence of administration involvement in the IRS's scandalous and illegal harassment and intimidation of conservative nonprofit activist groups. We do know, however, that the scandal followed months of coordinated and unprecedented attacks by the administration and leading Democrats on private citizens and private advocacy groups for exercising their First Amendment rights in opposing Obama administration policies. The administration's investigation of the IRS's illegal behavior, perhaps the worst domestic political scandal since Nixon's Watergate, has been cursory at best.

Meanwhile, despite firm promises from *candidate* Obama that he would limit the scope of the president's national security power, *President* Obama's approach has been similar to his predecessor's.[12] National Security Agency collection of data on Americans has continued, and apparently did not trouble Obama until rogue NSA contractor Edward Snowden leaked relevant documents and caused a public uproar over the scope of the program.

So much for our first civil libertarian president. Hope sprang eternal for some, though. In 2012, Rosen admitted, "I was wrong, and the last three years have offered plenty of disappointments in the president's record on privacy and national security." "But," he added, "if Obama wins a second term, I hope reelection gives him the freedom to redeem that unfulfilled promise."[13]

If anything, though, from a constitutional perspective Obama's second term has been even worse than his first. Civil libertarian and separation of powers dreams have met the continued harsh reality of the Obama administration's rampant lawlessness. Many of us, including very smart and sophisticated observers like Rosen, fell for a rhetorical con job when Obama was running for president back in 2008. As Obama's consistent record shows, and as this book thoroughly documents, it turns out that our constitutional law professor-in-chief and his high-level appointees simply never cared much about respecting the Constitution and the rule of law.

LAWLESS

Chapter 1

WHY SO LAWLESS?

EVEN AS THE PARTISAN POLITICAL DIVIDE continues to widen, one thing has long united Democratic and Republican presidents—aggressively expanding presidential prerogatives at the expense of Congress. Presidents are naturally inclined to test the legal and political limits of their power. In part, this is because politicians naturally desire to get as much political power as they can. But in part, it's because the Constitution's original design has been upended by the evolution of American politics.

Congress, not the president, is supposed to have primary responsibility for most lawmaking. In practice, however, the public gives the president credit and assigns him blame for everything that happens under his watch. Presidents want to have as much control as possible over their political fate, even if that means illegally expanding their own authority at the expense of Congress.

Moreover, Congress has found it politically convenient to pass vague, broad laws. Those laws give the president and his underlings the authority to work out the details, providing many opportunities for abuse. Finally, the rise of the United States as the greatest military power in the world has concentrated power in the president because he is the commander-in-chief of the

American military. Congress, meanwhile, has rarely tried to limit this power.

The result, since at least the Theodore Roosevelt administration in the early twentieth century, has been an ever-expanding "imperial presidency." Congress enacted a series of reforms in the 1970s after the Watergate scandal and the Vietnam War to try to curb presidential excesses and reassert Congress's authority. These reforms have been largely ineffective, and the president's power has continued to grow under both Democratic and Republican presidents.[1] The George W. Bush administration was especially aggressive in claiming unilateral authority over military and foreign affairs.

To some extent, then, the Obama administration has simply continued trends inherited from its predecessors. Obama, however, has asserted broad presidential prerogative across an unusually wide range of policy areas. As one liberal law professor puts it, "while Obama did not create the uber-presidency, he has pushed it to a new level of autonomy and authority."[2] Given prior expansions of presidential power, we may soon reach a tipping point where the constitutional balance of power is totally and permanently out of whack and presidents gain quasi-dictatorial powers.

When other presidents have tested the limits of their power, they have generally been responding to a major domestic or foreign crisis—the Civil War, World War I, the Great Depression, World War II, and 9/11, for example. Obama's mantra, by contrast, has been that "we can't wait" for Congress to act on a wide range of domestic and foreign policy items. Most of these were emergencies only in the sense that Obama was desperate to reward loyal political constituencies.[3]

One reason the Obama administration has been so assertive is that he's the first president in decades who won after running openly as a dove on foreign policy and a liberal on domestic policy. When Obama was elected, progressives believed that after decades in the political wilderness their moment had finally arrived; they were going to control American politics indefinitely and use that power to permanently transform society.

Hopes for progressive hegemony were dashed by the Republicans' stunning takeover of the House of Representatives in the 2010 election. This was widely seen as a reaction to the Obama administration's big-government policies in general, and the Affordable Care Act in particular. Nevertheless, Obama did win two presidential elections, and he, his administration, and their supporters have been intent on institutionalizing whatever progressive policies they can. Given the decades-long liberal goal of nationalizing health care, they are especially intent on preserving Obamacare, even if it means acting illegally.

The obvious downside for progressives is that the Obama administration is creating dangerous precedents that can be used and abused by future presidents, including conservative Republican presidents. But Obama and his advisors refuse to subordinate their short-term political and ideological goals to the long-term goal of preserving the broad principles animating our legal and constitutional system. While politicians often don't look beyond their own success or failure, it's still surprising just how neglectful of legal norms Obama has been, especially given his campaign promises to respect the Constitution and his background teaching constitutional law for many years at the University of Chicago.

Part of the problem is that Obama faces a significant ideological barrier in keeping his campaign pledges. He and many of his administration's top lawyers come from an intellectual tradition that is very skeptical of traditional notions of the rule of law and constitutional fidelity.

On the constitutional front, liberals and progressives have long argued that there is no objective meaning to the Constitution, that theories of interpretation focusing on the Constitution's original, objective meaning are nonsense, and that the Constitution is a "living" document that must evolve with the times. This view sometimes seems to merge with a crass legal realism that holds that all law is politics. If so, there is little reason to value constitutional fidelity—indeed, the concept itself becomes unclear—or to adhere to a fixed understanding of particular constitutional provisions. Constitutional politics becomes reduced to plain politics, and the meaning of the Constitution becomes whatever can advance one's political agenda.

The Obama administration's actions also reflect long-standing progressive unease with the concept of the rule of law. The "rule of law" is maintained by following the law in ways that promote consistency and stability—and by ensuring equal treatment of parties. It requires both judges and law-enforcement officials to act impartially and without abusing their power.

The rule of law was once considered the key element of left-liberal theories of justice, but no more. Consider that the leading liberal lawyers' organization, the American Constitution Society, proclaims that its mission is to promote the "vitality of the U.S. Constitution and the fundamental values it expresses: individual rights and liberties, genuine equality, access to justice, democracy, and the rule of law."[4] The rule of law is given no more weight than amorphous ideological goals like "genuine equality."

A key aspect of the rule of law in the American constitutional system is the separation of powers. The legislative branch (Congress) makes the law, the executive branch (the president) sees to it that the laws are faithfully executed, and the judicial branch (the courts) is charged with applying the law to particular civil and criminal cases. The president oversteps his bounds and violates the rule of law when he tries to assert a power given to another branch. This happens most often when he tries to make law himself rather than enforce laws enacted through the normal legislative process. A related violation of the rule of law occurs when the president refuses to fulfill his explicit constitutional responsibility to "faithfully execute" laws that are on the books.

The importance, and even coherence, of the concept of the rule of law came under a series of attacks in the legal academy from the left starting in the mid-1970s. First came the Critical Legal Studies movement (CLS). CLS is an intellectual descendant of the Legal Realist movement of the pre–World War II period. In its crudest version, realists argued that laws and judicial precedents are so indeterminate that they could mean whatever interpreters want them to mean. In less crude versions, legal realism meant that extralegal considerations such as the economic or class interests of judges and legal scholars affect legal interpretation far more often and to a much greater extent than legal scholars typically recognized.

Legal realism fell out favor after World War II, as it seemed nihilistic and the type of theory that gave aid and comfort to totalitarians like the Nazis and Communists by undermining the rule of law. But realism made a strong comeback in three forms in the 1970s.[5] Realism's fondness for basing legal decision-making on empirical studies rather than on legal precedent influenced the law and economics and law and society movements. Meanwhile, a radical critique of law extrapolated from legal realism found a home in the CLS movement, which was organized and promoted by young, left-wing academics.

As law professor Charles Barzun explains, CLS adherents "argued that the rule of law was both impossible in practice and, in any event, undesirable in theory."[6] The invitation for the first CLS conference held in 1977 declared that "law is an instrument of social, economic, and political domination, both in the sense of furthering the concrete interests of the dominators and in that of legitimating the existing order."[7] The more general sensibility of the movement can be summed up with the mantra,

"Law is politics." If that's what you think of law, the concept of the rule of law obviously won't appeal to you. And indeed, CLS advocates argued that traditionalist legal scholars were hiding behind the notion of the rule of law to disguise their political choice to defend an unjust status quo.

CLS's attack on the rule of law informed two additional movements: radical legal feminism and critical race theory (CRT). Like CLS advocates, radical legal feminists argue that the concept of the rule of law legitimizes and reinforces injustice, particularly a status quo of male domination.[8] Critical race theorists, meanwhile, believe that supposedly objective standards like the rule of law and adherence to legal precedent mask a system that supports continued white racial dominance. CRT ultimately had a very similar bottom line to CLS. "If there is any central message of CRT's radical multiculturalism," law professors Daniel Farber and Suzanne Sherry conclude, that message is "it's all politics."[9]

The various groups of critical scholars—whose influence peaked just when Barack Obama was attending Harvard Law School—were and are a minority even among left-leaning (that is, the vast majority of) law professors. Nevertheless, their influence has been broadly felt. First, critical theory has helped erode commitment on the legal left to freedom of speech, due process, and other core civil liberties protected by the Constitution and once considered by liberals to be essential to the rule of law.

"Crits" denigrate these rights as a throwback to atavistic "liberal" (in the philosophical sense of believing in rights against the government) individualism. As a leading "critical" scholar emphasized, CLS "is not committed at any level to liberalism."[10] Protecting rights, crits argue, is just one political choice among many, and there is no reason to privilege that choice over more pressing competing goals, such as promoting an egalitarian society.

Meanwhile, while modern progressive thinkers have not formally abandoned commitment to the rule of law, to many the concept no longer stands for such values as objectivity and consistency, for a government of laws and not men. Instead, the rule of law is taken to mean "before the government can do something we favor, we must find some not-completely-absurd interpretation of existing law that allows us to do it." This puts some constraint on what the government can do, as the law will stretch only so far before breaking. Ultimately, however, this resembles the rule of clever and politically willful lawyers more than the rule of law as traditionally conceived.

Government officials wanting to stretch their power as far as they can without blatantly violating the law is hardly news. What is news, however, is that top Obama administration officials have seen this not as something to be ashamed of, but as a *desirable* way of governing; something to brag about rather than do surreptitiously. Obama behaves as if there is some inherent virtue in a president ignoring the Constitution's separation of powers in favor of presidential decree, as if promoting progressive political ends at the expense of the rule of law is proper not simply as a desperate last resort but as a matter of principle.[11] After all, Obama says, democracy is unduly "messy" and "complicated."[12]

Worse yet, as George Washington University law professor Jonathan Turley writes, the Obama "administration acts as if anything a court has not expressly forbidden is permissible."[13] In many situations, no one has legal standing to challenge the president's actions in court—which means that no judge can stop the lawbreaking.

Obama and his allies no doubt would pose the dilemma this way, in the context of the illegal measures the president has taken to prop up Obamacare: "If we can find a way to ensure that millions of Americans are not deprived of health insurance, shouldn't we find a way to do so?" This sort of ends-justifies-the-means reasoning is understandable to the extent that it reflects a sincere desire to use the government's resources to help needy Americans. However, it neglects the long-term damage of undermining legal restraints on the president in favor of protecting a current political agenda, however worthy that agenda seems to its advocates. "We had no choice but to seize power to help the people" is exactly the rhetoric and reasoning used to justify tyranny around the world.

Ultimately, the Obama administration's cavalier attitude toward the rule of law can only be justified if one thinks that law is just politics by another name. If that's what Obama and his appointees believe, perhaps the crits have won after all.

Ideology aside, another reason that President Obama has been especially aggressive in pursuing illicit initiatives is that he has been able to get away with it. Previous presidents who engaged in wrongdoing have had members of their own political party who were willing to stand up and criticize them. Many Republicans turned on Richard Nixon as the Watergate scandal unfolded. More recently, Democratic Senator Joe Lieberman strongly criticized Bill Clinton for carrying on an affair in the White House and then lying under oath about it, and John McCain strongly opposed the Bush administration's policy of waterboarding high-level terrorist detainees.

But with Washington politics more polarized than it has been since the Civil War—in part because unlike for most of American history, the Democrats and Republicans have so clearly divided into a progressive and a conservative party, respectively—one can't count on partisans for one side to criticize their own. And when members of the opposing party raise legitimate concerns about the legality of the president's actions, it's all too easy for the public to dismiss those concerns as mere partisan sniping.

High-level Democratic politicians not only have generally failed to criticize Obama administration lawlessness but also have often encouraged it. For example, in his 2014 State of the Union address, Obama promised to circumvent Congress to achieve his policy goals. Instead of defending Congress's turf, House and Senate Democrats responded with a standing ovation.[14]

The traditional media establishment—newspapers like the *New York Times* and *Washington Post*, National Public Radio, and the three major TV network news operations, often referred to as the "mainstream media"—could have served as a check on the Obama administration's abuses. Even though these news organizations have long been associated with a liberal political outlook, they once had a professional ethos that encouraged them to ferret out political scandals whether the source was Republican or Democratic.

The establishment media, however, has largely given up its role as an independent watchdog. Liberal reporters and news editors, i.e., the great majority of reporters and news editors, are less willing to put their ideology aside, and more willing to exhibit partisanship in favor of President Obama and the Democrats.

An important factor in the decline in nonpartisan investigative zeal among establishment reporters is that well-paying jobs in journalism have been decimated, and working in politics has emerged as an important career alternative. Given that journalists who cover national politics are overwhelmingly Democrats, working in politics means working in Democratic politics, including potentially serving in the Obama administration. Jay Carney, for example, went from being *Time* magazine's Washington bureau chief to running Vice President Biden's communications operation. He ultimately served as President Obama's press secretary. The career-driven need to keep good relations with the White House and prominent congressional Democrats inhibits hard-hitting journalism.

Political ideology, of course, has also played a significant role in the decline of the media's watchdog role. Reporters have long leaned liberal, but they increasingly grow up, go to college, and work in "deep blue" liberal environments where liberal Democrats are presumptively the good guys and conservative Republicans the bad. Former CBS correspondent Sharyl Attkisson was one of the few journalists not working for a conservative outlet who seriously investigated Obama administration scandals such as Benghazi, Fast and Furious, and Solyndra. For her efforts, she got a tongue-lashing from various administration officials, the silent treatment from administration spokespersons, hacking of her personal and work computers by the government, attacks from administration partisans like Media Matters, and, crucially, the contempt of her liberal CBS colleagues.[15]

Attkisson eventually felt "marginalized and underutilized" at CBS,[16] and left. Attkisson later told CNN that some managers at CBS News are "so ideologically entrenched that . . . they have a difficult time viewing a story that may reflect negatively upon government or the administration as a story of value."[17] And if media elites are not willing to encourage their reporters to cover "sexy" Obama administration scandals, they surely are not going to express much interest in the administration's steady and often subtle undermining of the Constitution and the rule of law.

Progressive "new media" outlets are even more partisan than establishment outlets are. As one former liberal blogger put it, "The incentives are to play ball, not to speak truth to power. More clicks. More action. Partisanship drives clicks."[18] The Obama White House has actively cultivated partisan bloggers, but White House perks come with an implicit threat: annoy the wrong people with your blogging, and you can find yourself on our enemies list—and forget about ever winning that dream job as a speechwriter for the vice president.

Obama has not gotten away scot-free, as the conservative media—from Fox News to the *Wall Street Journal*'s editorial pages to Rush Limbaugh and other radio talk shows to hundreds of blogs—have relentlessly followed and criticized Obama's scandals, including the constitutional ones. But the increased prominence of conservative media may have had the perverse effect of making reporters for mainstream liberal outlets more hesitant to criticize the president. This is partly because they fear contributing to what they see as a right-wing feeding frenzy, and partly because establishment outlets may feel less responsibility to cover a story if conservative media are doing so.[19]

Arrogance is also a factor in the Obama administration's lawlessness. All presidents are arrogant; no humble person gets up one morning and says to himself, "I really think I should be the leader of the free world." Obama is no exception. In 2006, he told a staffer: "I think that I'm a better speechwriter than my speechwriters. I know more about policies on any particular issue than my policy directors. And I'll tell you right now that I'm gonna' think I'm a better political director than my political director."[20] But the Obama administration's arrogance is pervasive. As a leading left-wing activist told the *Huffington Post*'s Sam Stein: "These guys are stunningly arrogant. They really believe that their shit doesn't smell, that they have all the answers. And that arrogance continues to hurt them."[21]

The source of this arrogance lies, at least in part, in the attitudes of post-1970s graduates of elite universities. Past generations of elite political types derived their sense of superiority from a WASPish Old Boy Network. The Obama generation of elite political liberals, including many of the president's top aides and appointees, believe in meritocracy. But their version of meritocracy is based not solely on demonstrated achievement, but also on where one went to college and graduate school— but only if one is on the left side of the ideological spectrum, as conservative or libertarian views mark even the most accomplished people as fools or knaves, if not both. The converse belief is that progressives are presumptively wiser and morally superior to their ideological opponents, which undermines any desire to compromise with them.

President Obama graduated from Columbia University and Harvard Law School. Many of his advisors went to similarly elite colleges and graduate schools. The political culture at these schools considered far-leftists to be within mainstream political discourse, but run-of-the-mill conservatives to be, at best, on the extremist fringe.

It's hard to exaggerate how far skewed to the left the political environment was at Harvard Law School and other elite law schools in Obama's day—even while most students eagerly lined up for high-paying jobs representing large corporations. As one Harvard Law School graduate, class of 1994, puts it, at Harvard "radical was mainstream and conservative was radical."[22]

I can attest to this from my years at the Yale Law School, which I attended from 1988 to 1991, exactly when Obama attended Harvard. At the time, Harvard was considered significantly less friendly to right-of-center students than was Yale. Nevertheless, a significant fraction of Yale law students actively shunned, encouraged others to shun, and sometimes tried to publicly humiliate, those classmates they deemed to be "reactionaries"—a category that included people with moderate or right-of-center political views that would be utterly mainstream almost anywhere else. Even the more fair-minded liberal students who were polite to, or even friendly with, their conservative and libertarian classmates— and Obama was very polite to his conservative classmates at Harvard[23]—accepted their classmates' hostility to non-left-wing peers as a mundane part of life at an elite Northeastern university.

Attending such institutions and then working in liberal Democratic politics inevitably gave Obama and his advisors of similar background a very slanted perspective on the "respectable" ideological spectrum. This perhaps explains how Obama, the most liberal president in decades, someone whose known intellectual influences were all on the left,[24] could tell supporters with a straight face, that "I'm not a particularly ideological person,"[25] or how biographer Chuck Todd can report that "nothing irks Mr. Obama more than the idea that he's somehow a leftist or liberal."[26] After all, at Harvard Law School, he was a moderate!

If being on the liberal left makes someone moderate, the corollary is that conservatives are extremists. Does Obama himself believe that? The evidence suggests that he does and that he is hardly the only one in his administration to feel that way. Consider Obama's response when journalist George Stephanopoulos asked Obama in April 2008 about his ties to Bill Ayers. Ayers is a far leftist who was involved in several domestic terrorist bombings in the 1970s. He told the *New York Times* in 2001, "I don't regret setting bombs, I feel we didn't do enough."[27] After downplaying his friendship with Ayers, Obama added, "I'm also friendly with Tom Coburn, one of the most conservative Republicans in the United States Senate,"[28] as if the law-abiding Oklahoma senator is somehow the right-wing extremist version of Ayers.

Even the Obama administration's friends have noticed its hostility to conservatives. Former Obama Secretary of Defense Leon Panetta has explained that President Obama sees congressional Republicans as "people that simply won't—don't wanna do the right thing for the country." Panetta expressed regret at Obama's failure to work with the GOP and added, "Well, the reality is, if you wanna govern in this country, you have to deal with people you don't like."[29] But if Obama really believes that congressional Republicans are extremists who are unwilling to cooperate with him even when they know it would be "the right thing for the country," it's not surprising that he prefers to try govern on his own.

And in fact, the Obama administration's defenders blame House Republicans' purported extremism for the president's failure to work with them. Yet the Republican leadership is no more conservative today than it was in the mid-1990s, when Bill Clinton found a way to work with the likes of Tom DeLay on major issues like welfare reform. Besides, in the American constitutional system, even blatant obstructionism from Congress does not give the president any additional authority. Given the separation of powers, a large risk of gridlock is built into the Constitution. As Professor Jonathan Turley notes, there has been bitter partisan division in Washington in the past, but no one thought that this somehow gave the president power to circumvent the lawmaking process.

In short, President Obama and many of his advisors are part of an elite liberal intellectual class whose members believe that fidelity to the Constitution and the rule of law are often less important than achieving progressive political ends. Obama came into office with a huge congressional majority, and what he and his supporters thought was a mandate to fundamentally move American society to the progressive left. Conservatives, however, have thwarted this ambition, especially since Republicans took control of the House of Representatives in the 2010 midterm elections. These same conservatives, meanwhile, are held in contempt by elite progressives, who think they are either dumb or evil, or both, but that they are certainly extremists. Faced with the prospect of compromising with them, as Bill Clinton did when the Democrats lost the House in 1994, Obama instead chose to unilaterally pursue as many of his policy goals as possible, the Constitution and other legal restraints notwithstanding. The media, rather than calling the Obama administration on its worst tendencies, has often served as its cheerleader. As a result, the Constitution and the rule of law have suffered.

Chapter 2

NO JUSTICE AT THE
JUSTICE DEPARTMENT

THE JUSTICE DEPARTMENT, run for most of the Obama administration by the president's friend and confidant, Attorney General Eric Holder, has enabled the Obama administration's lawlessness. This enabling was sometimes direct. Several times the Justice Department filed briefs asking the Supreme Court to adopt outlandish legal theories that pleased important Democratic constituencies but were rejected by 9–0 votes in the Supreme Court.[1] The Department also failed to cooperate with congressional investigators engaging in normal oversight of the administration's activities—so much so that Holder was the first attorney general to be held in contempt of Congress. Holder's behavior was sufficiently troubling that even most House Democrats declined to vote against the contempt resolution.[2]

Beyond that, rather than setting a good example for the rest of the administration that the rule of law trumps politics, Holder accelerated the Justice Department's creeping politicization. Holder showed his lack of concern for legal niceties very early in the Obama administration. In April 2009, less than three months after Inauguration Day, the administration decided to push for a law that would grant Washington, D.C., an elected, voting representative in the House of Representatives. The Constitution, however, limits formal representation in Congress to the "citizens of the several states." D.C. is designated a special federal enclave, and is not a state or part of a state and therefore may not have a voting representative in Congress.[3]

The Justice Department had affirmed and reaffirmed this understanding of the Constitution repeatedly over the decades through formal opinions offered by the Office of Legal Counsel, a group of White House lawyers hired to give the president sound, objective legal advice. OLC attorneys, as part of the executive branch of government, try very hard to find legal support for the president's policies. Attorneys at Obama's OLC nevertheless objected to the D.C. voting bill, citing OLC memos dating back decades as well as the plain text of the Constitution.

Instead of deferring to the OLC, Holder took the highly unusual step of seeking a second opinion from lawyers in the Solicitor General's office. Holder did not ask the SG's office if the law was constitutional, because he knew the answer would almost certainly have been a strong "no." Instead, he asked whether the lawyers in the SG's office would be able to defend the law in court. The SG's office, by tradition, will defend any federal law in court, so long as the defense is not entirely frivolous. Given that very lenient standard, the SG's office told Holder it would defend the law if passed.[4] Holder then gave the president the legal green light to endorse the voting bill.

Very little was at stake. Even if the proposed law had passed, the D.C. representative's vote would almost never have been decisive. If such a vote ever did break a tie, any law passed because of that vote would have immediately been challenged in court. A judge would then almost certainly have invalidated the law because the deciding vote was cast by someone whom the Constitution bans from voting in Congress.

In other words, the D.C. voting bill was purely symbolic, a mere sop to liberal constituency groups that have been unsuccessfully pushing for D.C. statehood and other ways of increasing the (overwhelmingly Democratic) District's political power. Holder was nevertheless ready and willing to undermine the OLC. This suggested right at the start of the administration that its advice would be ignored and overridden whenever it might impede the administration's desired political goals.

The OLC rebuffed the administration again when it advised the president that he could not ignore the War Powers Resolution when it resorted to military force in Libya (see chapter 3). This led Obama to appoint Virginia Seitz to run the OLC. Seitz was expected to be more likely than her predecessor to tell the president what he wanted to hear.[5] The Senate confirmed Seitz in June 2011, and she soon lived up to expectations.

Seitz's OLC issued an opinion that supported the legality of one of Obama's most egregiously unconstitutional actions. The Constitution provides that the president may temporarily appoint someone as a "recess appointment" when the Senate is in recess. The Senate, in part due to growing partisan bitterness in Washington, has became increasingly assertive of its power to refuse to consent to high-level presidential appointments. During the Republican George W. Bush administration, Democratic Senate Majority Leader Harry Reid held so-called pro forma sessions in which every several days a senator would open the Senate and then adjourn, usually, but not always, without conducting business. The Senate was not in official recess during these sessions, and the president therefore could not make a recess appointment.

This frustrated the Bush administration, and led to discussions within the administration about whether the president could declare the pro forma sessions to be illegitimate, and the Senate to really be in recess. If so, the president would have the power to make recess appointments even though the Senate was not officially in recess. The OLC conducted some preliminary research into the issue, but the Bush administration never pursued it.

The Obama administration, as we shall see, was much more willing to push the limits of the recess appointments power. From the start it sought to use recess appointments not just to overcome Senate resistance to confirming President Obama's nominees but also to avoid potentially embarrassing Senate confirmation hearings. For example, Obama used a recess appointment to install Donald Berwick to run the Center for Medicare Services. Given that Democrats had a large majority in the Senate, Berwick almost certainly would have won a confirmation battle.

The problem was that Berwick had praised Britain's health care system, which is a "single-payer" system run and paid for by the government.[6] A fleshing out at a confirmation hearing of Berwick's views on the government's proper role in health care delivery might have undermined the moderate image the administration was trying to project on health care. On December 2, 2011, Berwick resigned because Republicans, having picked up seats in the Senate in the 2010 elections, had enough votes to block a formal nomination, and his recess appointment was about to expire.[7]

The Obama administration went even further with recess appointments later in Obama's first term. The Republican minority blocked several major appointments through filibusters, and, with the help of the Republican-controlled House, kept the Senate in pro forma session. In retaliation, the Obama administration announced three recess appointments on January 4, 2012, two to the National Labor Relations Board and one to run the new Consumer Financial Protection Bureau. President Obama told the media, "We can't wait to act to strengthen the economy and restore security for our middle class and those trying to get in it, and that's why I am proud to appoint these fine individuals to get to work for the American people."[8] Two days later, Seitz's OLC issued an opinion that the president could reasonably decide that the Senate is not really in session when it was holding pro forma sessions.[9] Almost no one found the OLC's reasoning persuasive.[10]

The administration's legal position was also undermined by the Senate's approval of an extension of a payroll tax cut during a pro forma session less than two weeks prior to the recess appointments, during the time that the OLC and the Obama administration argued that the Senate was in recess. The president signed the bill. It's absurd to argue, as the administration implicitly did, that the Senate was in recess for the purpose of recess appointments, but was not in recess for the purpose of considering and voting on legislation.[11] As law professor Jonathan Turley scolds, "The fact that the administration decided to force a confrontation on such a weak case shows not just a lack of judgment but a cavalier attitude towards the costs of such losses."[12]

The Supreme Court ultimately had an opportunity to judge the constitutionality of the recess appointments undertaken when the Senate was in pro forma session. Solicitor General Donald Verrilli gamely tried to argue to the Court that when the Senate refuses to confirm presidential nominees, and that refusal interferes with the working of government, the president's appointment power must expand to ensure that he can faithfully execute the laws.[13]

The justices didn't buy it. Justice Samuel Alito told Verrilli that if presidential appointment power expanded because of an irresponsible or intransigent Senate, this had "nothing whatsoever to do with whether the Senate is in session or not." Justice Elena Kagan added that the recess appointments power was not meant to deal with mere stubbornness by the Senate. Verrilli then acknowledged that he was arguing that regardless of the original meaning of the recess appointments power, it "may now act as a safety valve" for Senate intransigence. Chief Justice John

Roberts retorted, "You spoke of the intransigence of the Senate. Well, they have an absolute right not to confirm nominees that the President submits." The president's remedy for nonconfirmation, Roberts suggested, is not to exercise unilateral power, but to nominate someone else the Senate is willing to confirm. A showdown between the president and the Senate, Justice Stephen Breyer chimed in, is a "political problem, not a constitutional problem."[14]

Not surprisingly, the Supreme Court held that Obama's purported recess appointments were unconstitutional and therefore void.[15] All nine justices agreed that the Senate, not the White House, gets to decide when the Senate is in recess, and that pro forma sessions in any event count as being in session because the Senate could, if it chose, conduct business during those sessions.

Meanwhile, Holder not only failed to depoliticize the problem-filled Justice Department's Civil Rights Division but also made things worse. Problems at the division went back at least to January 2001. Outgoing Clinton administration lawyers, worried that the incoming Bush administration would move the division's policies to the right, engaged in a frenzy of hiring, done in irregular ways, to fill civil service positions with liberals before the Bush administration took over.

These lawyers were hired to help stymie Bush administration priorities, and that's what they did. Frustrated by the civil servants' lack of cooperation, Bush administration officials tried to hire more compliant attorneys. They did so by deliberately seeking out attorneys with conservative political views. Implicitly considering ideology in hiring civil service attorneys for the Civil Rights Division was hardly new, albeit illegal; unlike political appointments, career civil service jobs are supposed to go to the most qualified applicants regardless of party affiliation or personal ideology. Bush officials nevertheless considered partisan affiliation and ideology when hiring civil servants. One result was that the Justice Department hired attorneys who had significantly less impressive credentials than was typical for the prestigious Civil Rights Division.[16] Democrats had a field day criticizing the Bush Justice Department for violating federal law by hiring lawyers based on their political background.

Meanwhile, many liberal career civil servants behaved badly, seeking to sabotage the lawful enforcement priorities of the Bush administration's senior appointees. In the Civil Rights Division's Voting Rights Section, tempers flared over whether the Voting Rights Act should be enforced in a race-neutral manner. The act as written protects the right of all Americans to vote. The Bush administration pursued both traditional enforcement actions investigating the possible suppression of minority voting and also cases involving white voters who allegedly faced discrimination in majority-black districts. Some progressive lawyers in the Voting Rights Section objected on principle to the latter cases, arguing that the purpose of the Voting Rights Act was to protect only minority voting rights. By bringing cases involving alleged discrimination against whites, the administration was diverting resources from the core purpose of the act. Progressive attorneys also resented the Bush administration's failure to challenge new state voter identification laws, which they argued were meant to discourage minority voter turnout.

Tensions between civil servants and political appointees are fairly common, especially when Republican appointees clash with the overwhelmingly liberal bureaucracy, but the career lawyers' reactions went way beyond normal bureaucratic infighting. Liberal lawyers harassed colleagues perceived to be conservative, including those hired well before the Bush administration arrived. The DOJ's Office of the Inspector General (OIG) later reported, for example, that one attorney "was ostracized and ridiculed, and had his work product copied from his computer files and distributed without his knowledge or permission, at least in part because of the perception that he was conservative and because of the legal positions he advocated while working on the submission."[17]

Some liberal employees posted on the Internet nonpublic information about goings-on in the Civil Rights Division, accompanied by a "wide array of highly inappropriate remarks ranging from petty and juvenile personal attacks to racist and potentially threatening statements."[18] A supervisor who became aware of such misconduct by one of his employees "not only suggested that the employee disregard counseling and admonishment from Division leadership, but also encouraged the subordinate to continue the improper conduct."[19]

When Eric Holder became attorney general, instead of closing down this ideological circus, he became the ringmaster. Holder and his underlings could have signaled an end to the ideological wars in the department, and a desire to depoliticize it, by continuing the prosecution of Bush-era cases brought in good faith by the previous administration that had a valid legal basis. Instead, out of a combination of ideological opposition to race-neutral enforcement of the Voting Rights Act and a desire to shift enforcement resources to the Obama administration's priorities, the Holder Justice Department made matters worse.

The first sign came when the Civil Rights Division failed to pursue a voter intimidation case arising from the November 2008 election. Video circulated on the Internet that showed two members of the thuggish New Black Panther Party standing outside a polling place in a majority-black precinct in Philadelphia dressed in paramilitary clothing, with one carrying a billy club. In January 2009, just before the Bush administration left office, the Civil Rights Division filed a civil lawsuit under the Voting Rights Act alleging illegal voter intimidation by both men.

In April 2009, the division essentially won the case by default because the defendants failed to appear in court. But the following month, the acting head of the Civil Rights Division reduced the scope of the complaint against the billy-club wielder so that the only consequence was an injunction banning him from carrying a weapon near a Philadelphia voting location through 2012.[20] Charges against the second man were dropped entirely.

Some have argued that, given limited prosecutorial resources and the rarity of voter intimidation prosecutions, the case should not have been brought to begin with. Despite the dramatic video, it's not clear that any voters were actually intimidated.[21] Nevertheless, once the case was successful, requiring only negligible additional resources to win a final court order, it was passing strange that the Justice Department declined to see it through.

The Obama administration denied that political appointees played any role in the disposition of the New Black Panther case. But the administration has not been able to explain a stream of emails that went back and forth about the case among senior Obama political appointees in the days before the Justice Department abandoned its prosecution.[22] These emails, a federal judge later wrote, "would appear to contradict" Assistant Attorney General (and future Secretary of Labor) Thomas Perez's sworn testimony before the US Commission on Civil Rights "that political leadership was not involved in that decision."[23]

The Justice Department's Office of Professional Responsibility ultimately investigated the department's handling of the case. Attorney General Holder told the *New York Times* while the investigation was still under way that "there is no 'there' there," and that the investigation was over a "made up controversy."[24] Given that Holder was the boss of the OPR employees undertaking the investigation, his public prejudgment compromised the investigation's integrity.[25]

The charitable explanation of the New Black Panther Party

fiasco is that the Obama administration was rebuking the Bush Justice Department. The new administration sought to send a somewhat juvenile message that "we think the Bush administration's prosecution priorities were so screwed up, we are not even going to pursue a case it was about to win." The Obama Civil Rights Division similarly dismissed a Bush-era lawsuit against the state of Missouri for failing to purge registration lists of deceased and no-longer-resident voters as required by the National Voter Registration Act of 1993.[26] The Obama administration sought to focus its resources on barriers to voting like voter ID laws, not on cleaning up voter lists.

Some former Bush officials, however, believed that the Justice Department's failure to pursue the New Black Panther Party case resulted from top Obama administration officials' ideological belief that civil rights laws only apply to protect members of minority groups from discrimination by whites. Department spokeswoman Tracy Schmaler denied any such motives. She asserted that "the department makes enforcement decisions based on the merits, not the race, gender or ethnicity of any party involved."[27] But an anonymous Justice Department official told the *Washington Post* that "the Voting Rights Act was passed because people like Bull Connor [a white police commissioner] were hitting people like John Lewis [a black civil rights activist], not the other way around."[28] The *Post* concluded that the New Black Panther Party case "tapped into deep divisions within the Justice Department that persist today over whether the agency should focus on protecting historically oppressed minorities or enforce laws without regard to race."[29]

The Office of Professional Responsibility's report on the case found that several former and current DOJ attorneys told investigators under oath that some lawyers in the Civil Rights Division don't believe that the DOJ should bring cases involving white victims of racial discrimination. The report also found that Voting

Section lawyers believed that their boss, appointed by President Obama, wanted them to bring only cases protecting members of American minority groups. She phrased this as having the section pursue only "traditional" civil rights enforcement cases. Her employees understood that by "traditional" she meant only cases involving minority victims.[30]

The boss in question claimed she was misunderstood, and that she was only alluding to a specific section of the Voting Rights Act that required certain states to get Justice Department "preclearance" before they modified their voting rules in a way that could potentially be deemed discriminatory. Since all voting rule changes affect one group or another in different ways, applying this rule to white voters as well as minority voters would require the section to spend significant resources preclearing *every* voting change in the affected states.

If there was, in fact, a misunderstanding, it was likely because the Obama/Holder Justice Department had provided ample reason to question whether it wanted to apply the law in a racially neutral manner. In addition to dropping most of the New Black Panther Party case, the department canceled an existing investigation into an alleged ballot theft in Noxubee, Mississippi, that benefited an African-American incumbent. Meanwhile, Holder himself made some racially charged comments, including suggesting that the controversy over the New Black Panther Party case demeans "my people," by which he meant African Americans.[31]

Meanwhile, the Obama Justice Department resumed civil service hiring for the Civil Rights Division based on illegal ideological criteria. In a 2008 speech to the liberal American Constitution Society, Holder had promised the Justice Department would be "looking for people who share our values," and that "a substantial number of those people would probably be members of the American Constitution Society."[32] As attorney general, Holder went about finding such people by looking for civil service candidates with a "commitment to civil rights."[33] Commitment to civil rights was in practice interpreted not as a commitment to enforcing the laws on the books, but as a commitment to left-wing political activism, as demonstrated by past work for liberal activist groups.

The result was rather astonishing. During the first two years of the Obama administration, over 60 percent of attorneys hired for civil service positions had liberal entries (such as working for a left-wing activist group) on their resumes and none had conservative entries.[34] The Justice Department's rationale for hiring progressive activist lawyers is that their "traditional civil rights backgrounds" gave them appropriate law-enforcement credentials.[35] In fact, few of the lawyers in question had much in the way of law-enforcement experience. Rather, much of their experience was in challenging existing law as insufficiently left-wing and advocating for new or amended laws. Yet, once hired by the Justice Department, they were charged with enforcing the same laws that they had been denouncing in press releases and friend-of-the-court briefs as oppressive, unjust, unfair, and racist.

For example, many attorneys hired by the Justice Department had worked for organizations that opposed any significant constitutional restrictions on government preferences in favor of members of minority groups. By contrast, existing Supreme Court precedent limits such preferences to very narrow circumstances. One top Obama appointee suggested that recent Supreme Court precedent on race preferences was analogous to *Dred Scott*, a notorious 1857 case that both endorsed nationwide slavery and held that people of African descent had no "rights the white man need respect."[36] Someone who so vehemently disagrees with the current state of the law is not best positioned to enforce it. Meanwhile, even when desperately searching for attorneys to fill new civil service positions, the Justice Department, for reasons it couldn't explain to investigators from the Office of the Inspector General, failed to contact experienced former Bush administration attorneys who could potentially have been lured back to the department.[37]

If all that isn't sufficient evidence to show illegal political bias in hiring in the Obama Justice Department, consider the Civil Rights Division's nonattorney civil service hires just in the Voting Rights Section. They had worked for left-wing activist groups, including the NAACP, the Stanford Immigrants Rights Project, the Lawyers Committee for Civil Rights Under Law, the American Constitution Society, the Urban Institute, the Asian American Justice Center, the "no human is illegal" campaign, and more.[38] It's hard to think of a good reason why a paralegal or other non-lawyer Civil Rights Division hire needed experience in an activist organization to do his job properly. But providing nonattorney employees at low-paying liberal organizations with government jobs is a tacit way of subsidizing those organizations. It signals potential employees of such organizations that they will have the inside track on higher-paying, more secure government jobs in Democratic administrations.

The Civil Rights Division is not the only highly politicized part of the Justice Department in the Obama administration. The Environment and Natural Resources Division is chock-full of left-wing attorneys.[39] Much of the Obama administration's environmental agenda has been stymied by opposition in Congress, including from Democrats. One work-around the administration hit upon is a tactic called "sue and settle." The Environment and Natural Resources Division encourages environmental groups to sue the government for purportedly lax interpretations of existing law. The parties then enter a settlement agreement that requires the government to regulate far more stringently than statutes and the formal regulation-writing process would allow. This allows the executive branch to engage in lawmaking without the approval or oversight of Congress or the public.[40]

Finally, there is the matter of the Justice Department's refusal to defend the Defense of Marriage Act (DOMA) from constitutional challenge.[41] For decades, attorneys general of the United States have taken the position that, regardless of their administration's own view of a law, "they will not call into question the constitutionality of any federal statute unless the law is so patently unconstitutional that no defense could be mounted in good conscience."[42] The Obama administration officially agrees with that long-standing principle.

In 2011, however, the Obama administration ignored that rule for political reasons. Challenges to DOMA, which defined marriage for federal purposes as consisting of a man and a woman to the exclusion of same-sex couplings, regardless of state law to the contrary, were working their way through the courts. With a tight 2012 reelection battle pending, and gay rights groups clamoring for the administration, which had still not announced its support for same-sex marriage, to show some goodwill, the administration refused to defend DOMA in court.

Attorney General Holder argued that the Justice Department could not in good conscience defend DOMA because there were no legitimate arguments to be made for its constitutionality. That was a rather implausible claim, given that the DOJ had defended DOMA in court just a year earlier. And recall that Holder's Justice Department had also taken the position that allowing D.C.'s representative in Congress to vote, in blatant violation of an explicit constitutional provision, was nevertheless "defensible."

The House of Representatives hired its own lawyers to defend DOMA, but the Supreme Court held it unconstitutional in a 5–4 decision. The fact that four of the nine justices thought DOMA to be constitutional shows that DOMA was not, in fact, so patently unconstitutional that one could not defend it in good conscience. As legal scholar Ed Whelan notes, both the Supreme Court majority and dissent criticized Holder for refusing to defend the law. Justice Anthony Kennedy, for the majority, complained that Holder's "failure to defend the constitutionality of an Act of Congress based on a constitutional theory not yet established in judicial decisions has created a procedural dilemma" and warned that such behavior "poses grave challenges to the separation of powers." In his dissent, Justice Antonin Scalia more bluntly opined, "There is no justification for the Justice Department's abandoning the law in the present case."[43] But there was, of course, a justification, just not a very good one; as has so often been true in the Obama administration, the president and his attorney general were more interested in playing politics and pursuing a progressive ideological agenda than in upholding the rule of law.

Chapter 3

A LEAVE OF
ABSENCE FROM THE
"REPUBLIC OF CONSCIENCE"

THE OBAMA ADMINISTRATION has been a huge disappointment to those who hoped President Obama would reverse the trend of presidents usurping more and more authority over foreign and military affairs. The Constitution provides only a broad, vague outline of presidential authority in these areas. The president gets to negotiate treaties (which then must be approved by two-thirds of the Senate) and is the commander-in-chief of the armed forces. Congress, meanwhile, has the exclusive power to declare war and to pass legislation regulating international trade.

The Constitution does not directly address any number of situations. For example, it does not say under what, if any, circumstances the president may, without Congress's consent, send armed forces into harm's way in a situation that does not amount to a formal state of war with another country.[1] Most scholars of the original meaning of the Constitution believe that the president was supposed to have only very limited authority to use armed force abroad without congressional consent. But for the last one hundred years or so, presidents have been sending soldiers to battle on their own say-so with very little pushback from Congress and the courts. Meanwhile, the Supreme Court has often suggested that the scope of a current president's power is defined in part by what his predecessors did.

Just about everyone acknowledges that the ultimate constitutional check on presidential authority was supposed to be Congress's authority to refuse to appropriate funds for the president's initiatives, the so-called power of the purse. The power of the purse worked reasonably well in America's early days, when the federal government was limited in scope and the president had to beg Congress for money before he could engage in major military action abroad.

Today, however, the power of the purse is no longer an effective constraint on the president, because the president has many ways to evade Congress's control over military appropriations.[2] Presidents have learned to use accounting tricks and loopholes to move funds Congress approved for one purpose over to a purpose Congress has not approved at all. Because of such manipulations, Congress never got the opportunity to decide whether to use its power of the purse to stifle US intervention in Libya in 2011. The Obama administration paid for that conflict entirely out of funds reallocated from other Defense Department accounts.[3]

The authors of the Constitution expected that Congress as a whole would be motivated to preserve its authority against presidential encroachment. The Founding Fathers, however, did not anticipate the development of our two-party system. At any given time around half the members of Congress belong to the same party as the president, and do not want to limit "their" president's authority.[4] Congress is therefore not likely to make a serious effort to close loopholes and forbid accounting tricks anytime soon.

Even if Congress did make more of an effort to use its power of the purse, it would not necessarily constrain the president. In 2014, Congress passed a law banning the president from using any Defense Department funds to release prisoners from Guantanamo Bay, Cuba, without giving Congress thirty days' notice. President Obama nevertheless traded five high-ranking Al Qaeda prisoners for captured US soldier Bowe Bergdahl without the required notice. This action blatantly violated both the 2014 law and the Antideficiency Act. The latter law forbids federal agencies to spend funds "in excess or in advance of amounts that are legally available." The nonpartisan Government Accountability Office concluded that the Obama administration violated a "clear and unambiguous law."[5] The administration floundered for a rationale for breaking the law, and never gave an entirely coherent explanation.

The decline in the importance of the power of the purse has removed an important congressional check on presidential abuse of power. Given that, to preserve the Constitution's intended balance of power, the president should err on the side of consultation and cooperation with Congress and shy away from unilateral action. Unfortunately, the trend has long been in the opposite direction.

While some people seem to think that aggressive use of presidential power was invented by the George W. Bush administration, Bush had nothing on Harry S. Truman. Truman involved the United States in a bloody, protracted, and unpopular war in the Korean peninsula under the authority of the United Nations, not Congress. Other presidents similarly ignored Congress, down to Bill Clinton, who intervened in Haiti and Kosovo without congressional assent.

The public mostly yawned over these violations of the separation of powers until the Bush administration. Bush, pushed by ideologues within the administration and by the felt necessity of countering Al Qaeda after 9/11, aggressively asserted presidential authority to act without Congress's permission, or even despite Congress's opposition. Among other things, this led to terrorism suspects, including American citizens, being locked up indefinitely without due process. Many Americans, especially civil libertarians both left and right, were outraged. Even within the administration, some lawyers thought Bush was taking things too far, and threatened to resign if the administration followed through on its most aggressive interpretations of the president's power over foreign and military affairs. The Supreme Court eventually took several opportunities to limit the president's power.

Obama ran as the anti-Bush, and that included rejecting the Bush administration's broad view of presidential power. Bush had argued that his inherent authority as commander-in-chief meant that he did not need Congress's permission to go to war in Iraq, though he obtained it anyway. By contrast, in response to a December 2007 *Boston Globe* survey of presidential candidates, Obama wrote, "The President does not have power under the Constitution to unilaterally authorize a military attack in a situation that does not involve stopping an actual or imminent threat to the nation."[6] Future vice president Joe Biden and future secretary of state Hillary Clinton, both running for president at the time, gave similar answers to the *Globe*.

Relying on campaign promises is, of course, foolhardy. Obama's statement, however, went beyond the usual campaign-trail hyperbole. Obama did not just criticize the incumbent administration, did not just promise to do better, but affirmed that he had a narrow *constitutional* vision of the scope of executive authority, a vision that would, if followed, limit his own authority as president. When Obama took the oath of office, Americans reasonably expected his sworn defense of the Constitution to include a refusal to order military action without Congress's backing unless there was an actual or imminent threat to the United States.

At first, it seemed like President Obama intended to stay true to the constitutional vision he promoted during his campaign. Soon after his inauguration, Obama told a group of liberal activists that he favored creating the legal and institutional conditions that would permanently limit the scope of presidential authority, especially with regard to counterterrorism. The participants couldn't believe their ears; a president willing to restrict his own power?[7] And the Obama administration did end or limit some of the Bush administration's most controversial policies.

Obama's reticence about presidential power, however, did not last long. For example, he vastly expanded the use of drone strikes to target Al Qaeda fighters otherwise beyond the reach of American forces in Pakistan, Yemen, and elsewhere.

The real moment of truth came in spring 2011, when Obama decided to intervene against Muammar Gaddafi's government in the Libyan civil war. No one, including the president, was bold or foolish enough to argue that the fighting in Libya, or the Libyan government itself, posed an imminent threat to the United States—the standard Obama had promised that he would abide by before committing US forces abroad without going to Congress first. Even the secretary of defense admitted that the war involved no "vital interest for the United States."[8] The best the Obama administration could come up with was that "the use of military force in Libya serves important U.S. interests in preventing instability in the Middle East and preserving the credibility and effectiveness of the United Nations Security Council."[9]

Obama needed to find legal authority for the intervention. Congress, and the Republican-controlled House of Representatives in particular, seemed disinclined to give the president explicit legal authority to intervene militarily in Libya. Obama, in turn, showing his usual disdain for House Republicans, refused to ask Congress for that authority. Some legal scholars, mostly conservatives, argued that intervening in Libya was well within the president's inherent authority as commander-in-chief. President Obama refused to take that tack. Doing so would have meant explicitly adopting a Bush administration–like theory of presidential power that would have alienated a substantial chunk of his core supporters. It also would have set a precedent that a Republican president could rely on in the future.

Instead, the Office of Legal Counsel issued a formal opinion letter defending the president's authority to use force in Libya.[10] The 1973 War Powers Resolution gives the president sixty days to notify and get the consent of Congress when involving American troops in "hostilities" abroad. The OLC opinion argued that this implicitly gives congressional assent to the president having unlimited war-making powers for those sixty days.[11] Not for the first time, a law meant to restrain executive power was instead used to justify expansive use of unilateral presidential authority.[12] Ironically, before State Department Legal Adviser Harold Koh joined the Obama administration, he had been one of the leading critics of this interpretation of the War Powers Resolution.[13] Koh, however, did not protest the OLC opinion.

The next problem the administration faced was that the Libya intervention, which it hoped would end before the sixty-day WPR deadline, dragged on. Adding to the pressure, Speaker of the House John Boehner sent a letter to President Obama pointing out that the president would be violating the War Powers Resolution unless he received congressional authorization by June 19.

As the deadline approached, Defense Department lawyers, though known for being hawkish on the scope of presidential authority, told the president that the WPR's requirements applied to the Libya intervention. The Office of Legal Counsel, which typically takes as aggressive a view of presidential power as a fair reading of the law would allow, also told the president that continued missile strikes would be covered by the WPR, and would have to stop absent congressional authorization.[14] Even Attorney General Holder endorsed this position.

Obama's response was to search for a lawyer in his administration who would opine that the War Powers Resolution didn't apply. Liberal Yale Law School professor Jack Balkin condemns such trolling as lawless. "The OLC's procedures," Balkin notes, "are designed to prevent precisely this sort of cherry picking. If the President can simply canvas the opinions of enough such lawyers he is not restrained very much by the law." Balkin was so disgusted that he referred to the president as "George W. Obama," the ultimate progressive insult.[15]

Obama was not obligated to listen to Defense Department lawyers, OLC lawyers, or anyone else.[16] Nevertheless, his refusal to be constrained by the first several groups of lawyers he consulted suggests a disdain for the law. After all, the president of the United States can almost always find *someone* in the government to tell him what he wants to hear.

Obama's quest for a malleable lawyer ended when he struck gold with Harold Koh. Koh, who exudes the persona of the friendly, rumpled professor, was a popular teacher at Yale Law School when I was a student there in the late 1980s. He later became dean, and, consistent with his own idealism and Yale Law's inimitable air of moral and intellectual smugness, proclaimed Yale's students to be "Citizens of the Republic of Conscience."[17] Koh's father, Kwang Lim Koh, was a South Korean diplomat who represented a democratic government, but resigned and sought asylum in the United States when a new regime took over in a coup. He told his son, "some people are eels. They slither where the power is. But it is the people who stick to their principles who can look themselves in the mirror."[18]

Koh made his academic reputation as a strong critic of what he deemed unconstitutional unilateral presidential action in foreign affairs. "For a quarter century before heading up State-

Legal," Harvard Law School's Jack Goldsmith notes, "Koh was the leading and most vocal academic critic of presidential unilateralism in war."[19] In Koh's book *The National Security Constitution*, he wrote that the president has exclusive powers only "with regard to diplomatic relations and negotiations and to the recognition of nations and governments." Otherwise, Koh argued, the Constitution gives Congress, and not the president, "a dominant role in the making of foreign policy."[20]

If anyone within the administration was going to challenge President Obama on executive power issues, Koh, with his idealism, strong preexisting views, and a cushy academic job waiting for him if he felt the need to resign, would have been the most likely candidate. In his opening talk to his State Department staff, Koh raised expectations that he would challenge the administration not just on legal issues but whenever he disagreed with a proposed policy. Koh told his staff their job was to "never say no, when our law and conscience say yes. But we should never, ever say yes, when our law and conscience say no." And what if the law says yes, but Koh and his staff thought a proposed policy was immoral, imprudent, or counterproductive? Such moral and practical judgments might seem beyond the job description of the Office of the Legal Adviser, but not to the former dean of the "Republic of Conscience." The Office of the Legal Adviser, Koh said, must "act as a conscience" and oppose "policies and practices that are 'lawful, but awful.'"[21]

And indeed, for the first year or so of the Obama administration, Koh acted as a "liberal gadfly" in the administration, just as his father's legacy, his academic record, and his speech to his staff would suggest.[22] He clashed with Defense Department officials who wanted to take more aggressive legal positions on presidential power than he supported, and with defense and political officials who opposed civilian trials for detainees captured in counterterrorism operations.[23]

Over time, though, Koh went native, adopting views of presidential power that surely would have shocked his pre–Obama administration self. He became one of the administration's most forceful advocates of using drone strikes to target alleged Al Qaeda figures. In fact, he sometimes found himself defending drone strikes to hawkish administration officials whom he had previously tangled with. These officials had seen Koh as a starry-eyed idealist, an amateur who was naïve about war and who failed to properly consider political constraints on the president.

Yet Koh wound up outhawking the hawks. Officials in the Defense Department and the CIA, who early in the Obama administration had been on the receiving end of Koh's moralizing, started privately mocking him as "killer Koh." Some drone operators considered printing T-shirts with the message: "Drones: If they're good enough for Harold Koh they're good enough for me."[24] Koh himself wondered how he went from being a very liberal law professor to helping determine which terror suspects should be killed in drone strikes.[25]

Before joining the Obama administration, Koh had argued that Congress's post-9/11 authorization of military force by the president was limited to attacking Taliban and Al Qaeda hideouts in Afghanistan and Pakistan. Once in the administration, however, Koh argued that Congress had authorized military action, including drone strikes, anywhere in the world against Al Qaeda. Despite the flip-flop, Koh's legal position was reasonable, if not inarguable. And unlike Bush administration claims of inherent executive power to make war, at least the legal authority the Obama administration claimed for drone strikes could be revoked at any time by Congress.

Critics claimed that the Obama administration was denying Al Qaeda fighters with American citizenship due process of law by killing them with drone strikes.[26] The administration and its defenders retorted that in wartime, it's irrelevant that an enemy combatant happens to have American citizenship.[27] No one, for example, argued that the US army had been obligated to try to avoid killing the thousands of World War II German soldiers who held American citizenship.[28]

Koh established criteria for drone strikes, ultimately endorsed by the Justice Department in a secret white paper.[29] These criteria arguably made sense from a policy perspective, but undermined his legal and constitutional arguments. First, Koh decreed that the United States could only use a drone strike against senior members of Al Qaeda, because only such individuals posed a unique threat to the United States.[30] If, however, the prevailing legal theory was that the United States was engaged in worldwide war against Al Qaeda and its affiliates, the United States should have been able to kill any Al Qaeda fighter, not just leaders.

Second, drone strikes were allowed only if there was evidence that the individual targeted was planning to strike at the United States.[31] Yet if the United States was truly at war with Al Qaeda, why, as a legal matter, did the military need to wait until an Al Qaeda fighter was planning an attack before he could be killed? Surely American forces could have bombed German soldiers on the Russian front in World War II, even though those particular soldiers posed no immediate threat to the United States.

To confuse matters further, the Obama administration put civilians in the National Security Council, a part of the White House bureaucracy, in charge of determining who would be targeted with drone strikes. In the normal course of a war, the uniformed military, subject to oversight by the president acting as commander-in-chief, decides what resources to use where. Relying on civilians to determine which enemy combatants to target, though not constitutionally prohibited, seems more appropriate for a law-enforcement action than for a war.

Allowing political appointees rather than the nonpartisan military to decide on targets raised concerns that targets could be chosen more for political than for strategic reasons. Famously, in a lengthy filibuster Senator Rand Paul raised the possibility that a president might eventually order drone strikes in the United States against alleged American domestic terrorists, which in turn could ultimately mean the president's political enemies. Some saw Paul's concerns as libertarian paranoia, but the administration fed them when Vice President Joe Biden described Tea Party Republicans as behaving "like terrorists," and a senior White House advisor referred to congressional Republicans as "suicide bombers."[32]

The administration also weakened its case by asserting that drone strike targets were getting "due process," just not "judicial process," because "internal deliberations in the executive branch" satisfied due process.[33] If Al Qaeda members targeted by the US military are the equivalent of enemy soldiers in wartime, as the US government asserts, regardless of citizenship they are not entitled to *any* process before a drone strike dispatches them. But if they fall into some other category that entitles them to due process, then they have a right to real due process, including arguing their case before a judge. Due process cannot be satisfied by a kangaroo-court procedure where the executive branch makes the rules, applies them, and executes punishment with no judicial oversight.[34]

When a plaintiff, the father of an American citizen who was targeted for a drone strike because of his role in Al Qaeda, tried to challenge the administration's position in an American court, the administration invoked the state secrets doctrine to get the case dismissed rather than publicly defend its legal theory.[35] All this makes one wonder if administration lawyers like Koh actually believed the "war with Al Qaeda" rationale they invoked.

Obama also put no external check on the process of determining who should be killed in drone strikes, nor did the administration publicly explain the legal reasoning behind, and the limits to, drone strikes. Indeed, the Obama administration argued that the legal memoranda that explained these things were "state secrets" that it would not divulge. The president implicitly asked the American people to trust the government with the unregulated and potentially unlimited authority to kill people.[36] Ironically, when George W. Bush was in office, future Obama attorney general Eric Holder forcefully denounced those who responded to concerns about the potential abuse of presidential power by saying "just trust us."[37]

In short, Koh and other Obama administration lawyers provided a confused legal rationale for drone strikes that ultimately had no principled basis, and gave the president extraordinary and potentially very dangerous power. The same, as we shall see, is true of Koh's rationale of why the president could ignore the War Powers Resolution when the United States bombed Libya.

Koh argued that extensive bombing strikes on Libya were not "hostilities" under the WPR "because they do not involve sustained fighting or active exchanges of fire with hostile forces, nor do they involve the presence of U.S. ground troops, U.S. casualties or a serious threat thereof."[38] In fact, US warplanes bombed Libya for weeks, and Libyan forces returned fire, though not successfully.

Koh's argument was rejected by legal scholars across the political spectrum. George Mason University law professor Ilya Somin deemed Koh's argument "barely worthy of response."[39] The Cato Institute's Gene Healy pointed out that "given that outrage over the illegal bombing of Cambodia was part of the backdrop to the WPR's passage, it would have been pretty strange if its drafters thought presidential warmaking was A-OK, so long as you did it from a great height."[40] Temple University law professor Peter Spiro opined that "if 'hostilities' are defined so as to include only really serious military engagements," then the WPR is "superfluous" because the Constitution requires congressional authorization for such engagements regardless of the WPR.[41]

Harvard's Jack Goldsmith added, "Common sense suggests that firing missiles from drones that kill people over an extended period of time pursuant to a U.N.-authorized use of force constitutes 'hostilities.' So too do standard definitions of the term 'hostilities.' "[42] Goldsmith also noted that a 1980 OLC opinion, which the Obama administration claims to accept, concludes that "the word hostilities was substituted for the phrase armed conflict during the subcommittee drafting process because it was considered to be somewhat broader in scope." The Libya intervention was clearly an armed conflict, so if "hostilities" is defined even more broadly than "armed conflict," the War Powers Resolution clearly applied.[43]

Even a younger Harold Koh would have utterly rejected the Obama administration's argument enunciated by an older Harold Koh. In *The National Security Constitution*, Koh criticized Congress for not challenging President Ronald Reagan's failure to invoke the WPR before bombing Libya in April 1986. In that operation, American war planes penetrated Libyan air space for all of twelve minutes. Koh nevertheless thought that it involved sufficient "hostilities" to implicate the WPR.[44]

Scholarly opposition to the administration's legal theory was not quite unanimous. Yale Law School professor Akhil Amar made the curious argument that the president complied with the WPR because "American forces are arguably not so much 'into' hostilities as 'above' them."[45] Beyond that, the strongest defense I have heard of Koh's reasoning came from a law professor sympathetic to the Obama administration. He told me that Koh's argument "wasn't completely ridiculous."

Koh later told the Senate that, in the spirit of the WPR, the administration consulted "extensively" with Congress before intervening in Libya. In fact, the administration primarily held discussions with a handful of important members of Congress it knew would support the intervention. Besides, the WPR requires not just "consultation," but congressional approval.[46]

In 2013, after Koh had left the government, President Obama decided to ask for Congress's assent before attacking Syria over its use of chemical weapons. With no such assent forthcoming, the president properly dropped the matter. This self-restraint was short-lived, however. When Obama decided to bomb ISIS positions in Syria and Iraq in fall 2014, he once again refused to ask for congressional permission, even though it almost certainly would have been forthcoming.

Koh's about-face on the scope of executive power raises the question of why he, unlike other Obama administration lawyers, agreed to endorse the ridiculous argument that bombing the heck out of Libya did not constitute "hostilities." It's one thing for someone to change his mind and become more hawkish on national security issues when he joins the government and is confronted with the reality of the threats facing the United States; it's quite another to change one's mind on what's *legal*, which should be consistent regardless of circumstances.

Perhaps Koh's long-standing objections to presidential unilateralism were primarily partisan sniping at Republican presidents. Koh is surely a partisan liberal Democrat. When he became dean at Yale Law School, conservative students and alumni observed a noticeable new chill coming from the law school administration.[47] A political partisan like Koh is less likely to object to executive action when the "good guys" are in charge than when the perceived miscreants on the other side are doing the same thing. In fairness to Koh, though, he did protest the planned deployment of American soldiers to Haiti during the Clinton administration in 1994. He wrote—ironically, as it turns out—that "nothing in the War Powers Resolution authorizes the President to commit armed forces overseas into actual or imminent hostilities in a situation where he could have gotten advance authorization."[48]

Maybe Koh just felt that concern over his own political future demanded that he justify what his boss, Secretary of State Hillary

Clinton, clearly wanted to do, which was intervene in Libya. Yale Law School professors, much less deans, are not exactly known for their modesty and lack of ambition, and Koh may have felt that crossing Clinton on this issue would cost him a high-level appointment in a future Hillary Clinton administration.

Koh has vehemently denied modifying his views for political reasons. The same month he advised the president that the War Powers Resolution does not apply to Libya, he told critics, "I never say anything I don't believe. Why should I? I have tenure. . . . If I quit this job I go back to a job where I have more job security, I work less hard, and I get paid a lot more. So I say that for this reason. If you hear me say something, you can be absolutely sure that I believe it, and [that includes] the administration's position on war powers in Libya."[49]

If we take Koh at his word, that suggests another explanation for his behavior. High-level political appointees who sell their souls for reasons of ambition or partisanship are a dime a dozen, and hypocrisy inside the Beltway runs as long and deep as the Potomac River. Koh's performance in the Obama administration, by contrast, may instead reflect that he's a true believer in a form of liberal internationalism that seeks to subordinate adherence to the American Constitution and the laws enacted under it to what its advocates consider the much more important values of international cooperation and humanitarianism.

We know from his writings that Koh believes that international norms may trump "American exceptionalism" as reflected in the Constitution, including the unusually broad protection of fundamental constitutional rights like freedom of speech that Americans enjoy.[50] Reactionary American nationalists, Koh has suggested, want to obey the Constitution, while forward-looking internationalists more wisely look to "international law and comity" to promote international legal institutions.[51] Therefore, for example, he suggests that American courts, instead of protecting hate speech under the First Amendment as they do now, should apply a "transnationalist approach to judicial interpretation" and allow such speech to be banned.

Allowing international law to trump ordinary American law presents an even easier case for Koh. Koh, like many progressive internationalists, believes that beyond self-defense against an attack from abroad, unilateral American military action generally violates international law. For example, in 2002 he argued that the United States could not lawfully invade Iraq unless it had the permission of the United Nations. American policy could turn on whether the government of Zambia, say, chooses to cast its deciding vote for or against proposed military action.

Meanwhile, many progressives believe American military action abroad that would be legally and ethically questionable if done for strategic reasons is fine and dandy if done to serve humanitarian goals. During the Clinton administration, many liberals who had consistently denounced previous American military action abroad warmly supported the administration's intervention in the former Yugoslavia, despite a lack of congressional approval. They approved of bombing Serbia in part *because* the United States had no obvious strategic stake in the conflict. The United States, therefore, was not "selfishly" elevating American interests over the interests of other nations, but was instead pursuing an internationalist, humanitarian agenda.

The Libyan intervention, then, was exactly the sort of war that a liberal internationalist like Harold Koh, if not the American public at large, could love. First, the war had the implicit backing of the United Nations, as the UN Security Council had unanimously passed a resolution establishing a no-fly zone over Libya.[52] It also had the backing of the Arab League, which also endorsed a no-fly zone.[53] Second, there was no discernible American strategic interest in intervening in Libya, and American intervention was justified primarily on humanitarian grounds. Finally, the United States did not act unilaterally in Libya, but acted through NATO and in alliance with Qatar. As NATO, and not the US military, took control of the operation, an anonymous Obama administration official proudly described the president's strategy as "leading from behind."[54]

If Libya had worked out (spoiler: it was a disaster), it could have set a new model for multilateral, UN-backed, humanitarian intervention, a dream of progressives going back to Woodrow Wilson and the League of Nations and beyond. Allowing the pesky War Powers Resolution to give Congress veto power over this potential achievement may simply have been something Harold Koh could not abide—especially when the House of Representatives was controlled by "reactionary," nationalistic Republicans skeptical of US military intervention in Libya. Why, after all, look "backward to territory and sideways toward executive power," when the government can instead rely on, as Koh has advocated, "transnational jurisprudence" that "looks forward toward political and economic interdependence and outward toward rules of international law and comity."[55] Why, indeed—other than the fact that the president takes an oath to uphold the American Constitution, not "rules of international law and comity."

Of course, President Obama, not Harold Koh, is ultimately responsible for the Obama administration's blatant violation of the War Powers Resolution. Given Obama's general disdain for nationalistic understandings of America's positive role in the world, and his preference for operating through multilateral organizations, he may have had the same reasons as Koh for being enthusiastic about the war in Libya.

Koh's transformation from an advocate of the strict separation of powers to an apologist for the Obama administration's abuse of executive power is nevertheless instructive. Many people wonder why progressive scholars and activists, who so intensely criticized the Bush administration for its broad and questionable exercises of presidential power in foreign and military affairs, have mostly been quiet about the Obama administration's similar actions. Indeed, one may wonder why the Obama administration's policies seem to have received so little resistance from within the administration, much less than the Bush administration's policies did. The answer lies in part in a combination of partisanship and desire born of ambition not to rile the powers-that-be. But as with Koh, also important is a sense that the Obama administration's lawlessness has been in service of the long-standing progressive dream of replacing traditional American nationalism with a multilateral humanitarianism, and, concomitantly, replacing loyalty to the US Constitution with American integration into a global constitutional and legal order beyond the control of the American polity.[56]

Chapter 4

THE ASSAULT ON PRIVATE PROPERTY AND FREEDOM OF CONTRACT

ENFORCING PRIVATE CONTRACTUAL ARRANGEMENTS, respecting private property rights, and fairly enforcing preexisting rules are crucial to the rule of law. If the government can simply change the rules governing private activity whenever it seems convenient or politically advantageous, and rewrite private contracts and take away people's property, a free society cannot flourish. A government with such power inevitably is tempted to abuse its authority and slide into despotism.

Until the 1930s, the Supreme Court placed significant limits on the ability of both federal and state governments to regulate private contracts and property rights. These limits tended to be broad and flexible, but they nevertheless inhibited abusive government policies. Most of these limits were abolished by the Court in a series of decisions starting in the 1930s. With economic progressivism ascendant, Americans were expected to place their faith in the political process to protect their economic freedom, and to expect that such freedom would often play second fiddle to whatever regulatory schemes the government decided to enact.

Still, the federal government obeyed some basic norms that respected private ordering. The government established and enforced bankruptcy laws that allowed creditors to know in advance what priority their claim on a debtor's assets would have if their loan went bad; never took a stake in private companies, lest that tempt them to interfere with corporate management; stayed out of private lawsuits when companies had allegedly injured the plaintiffs; and allowed companies to locate wherever they found the tax, regulatory, and labor climate to be most favorable.

Unfortunately, the Obama administration has violated all these norms, and also has the worst record on respecting property rights of any presidential administration. We'll get back to the property rights cases later. Let's start, instead, with the Obama administration's decision to ignore the law when it helped Chrysler and General Motors recover from the Great Recession of 2008.

The George W. Bush administration established the Troubled Asset Relief Program, or TARP, at the height of the 2008 financial crisis. TARP authorized the secretary of the US Treasury "to purchase . . . troubled assets from any financial institution, on such terms and conditions as are determined by the Secretary."[1] In December 2008, the Bush administration asked Congress for money to bail out Chrysler and GM. The House went along, but the Senate refused.

In a foreshadowing of the Obama administration, the Bush administration argued that Congress's refusal to rubber-stamp the president's proposal justified unilateral, illegal action by the president. Bush took $17 billion out of the $700 billion TARP fund to loan to the car companies, even though the fund was only supposed to be used for "financial institutions." A White House spokesman justified this presidential power grab by explaining, "Congress lost its opportunity to be a partner because they couldn't get their job done."[2]

The government then gave GM and Chrysler ninety days to

come up with viable turnaround plans. By the time the deadline arrived, the Obama administration was in office and neither company had made significant progress. Obama's underlings ordered Chrysler to merge with Italian automaker Fiat. Meanwhile, Steven Rattner, Obama's "car czar," ordered GM CEO Rick Wagoner to resign. Given GM's dependence on TARP money, Wagoner had no choice. So an unelected government bureaucrat, one not even confirmed by the Senate, fired the CEO of a major American company. At the same time, the Obama administration more than tripled the amount of TARP funds available to GM, without congressional approval.[3]

Rattner also forced out GM's acting chairman and personally recruited its new chairman. Rattner and his automobile industry task force—run by Brian Deese, a thirty-one-year-old Yale Law School student with no formal training as an economist and no experience in the automobile industry, or in any business, for that matter[4]—made all major business decisions for GM, including which brands to keep and which dealerships it should shed and how quickly it should shed them. For public consumption, the task force pretended that GM was acting autonomously. Rattner later complained that "as we drafted press statements and fact sheets, I would constantly force myself to write that 'GM has done such and such.' Just once I would have liked to write 'we' instead."[5]

Needless to say, a law that provided for the bailout of "financial institutions," however broadly construed, did not give Rattner and Deese the power to make day-to-day business decisions for GM. Rattner not only didn't care, he reveled in the lawlessness. The auto industry rescue, he wrote, "succeeded in no small part because we did not have to deal with Congress." If he had not been able to act unilaterally, he added, "we would have been subject to endless congressional posturing, deliberating, bickering, and micromanagement, in the midst of which one or more of the troubled companies under our care would have gone bankrupt."[6] Either that, or the Obama administration could have followed the law, and cooperated and compromised with Congress—which had a huge Democratic majority inclined to go along with the administration's initiatives.

Meanwhile, neither GM nor Chrysler had adequately prepared for bankruptcy, hoping that government handouts would be forthcoming. The Obama administration instead ordered both companies into bankruptcy, on pain of losing crucial federal financing.

Chrysler and GM could have gone through normal bankruptcy and reorganization proceedings. Many large American companies, including most major airlines, have done so. Both companies would likely have needed government financing for reorganization, given the credit crunch that came along with the financial crisis. But beyond a federal line of credit, neither company needed extraordinary and extralegal assistance. George Mason University law professor Todd Zywicki notes that GM was "practically a poster child" for a normal reorganization under Chapter 11 of the bankruptcy code.[7]

The Obama administration, however, rejected normal bankruptcy proceedings because they would have undermined the companies' obligations to union pension plans, and threatened unionized automobile workers' unusually generous salary and benefits packages. The autoworkers union was a huge supporter of both President Obama and the Democratic Party more generally in the 2008 elections, so the union's needs were an administration priority. The result was, according to Zywicki, an unprecedented process: "bankruptcy combined with a bailout, incorporating the worst elements of both."[8] The bankruptcy involved creating new legal entities—"new Chrysler" and "new GM." The government took a big stake in each.

As in normal bankruptcy, the shareholders in both companies lost almost everything.[9] But in a process very different from normal bankruptcy, the Obama administration managed Chrysler's bankruptcy so that the United Auto Workers union's benefit fund, an unsecured creditor, received forty cents on the dollar. Secured bondholders, who were by law to be paid in full before unsecured creditors received anything, received less, only twenty-nine cents on the dollar.[10]

Secured creditors are also normally entitled to a continuing claim on the reorganized company's assets to help repay the unpaid debt, a so-called deficiency claim. The Obama administration arranged instead for a transaction in which all of Chrysler and GM's assets were sold to new Chrysler and new GM, so that the old companies officially no longer had any assets.[11] Such a transaction, done without the approval of creditors, is ordinarily considered an illegal "sub rosa plan." The Obama administration did it anyway.[12] Car czar Rattner told a representative of Chrysler's secured creditors that "we have other plans for" Chrysler's assets—other than paying the secured creditors what they were entitled to by law, that is.[13]

Most holders of significant amounts of Chrysler secured debt agreed to the reorganization because as a practical matter they could not object. These bondholders were large financial firms like Citigroup and Goldman Sachs that needed assistance from the Obama administration because of the financial crisis. Also, their executives faced potential personal civil and criminal penalties for their behavior during the financial bubble that led to the Great Recession—but only if the Obama administration chose to go after them. Senior management wisely concluded that it was well worth taking a loss on their Chrysler debt holdings if that would placate the politicians who controlled their fate.

Hedge fund bondholders with no regulatory issues to worry about wanted to oppose the illegal reorganization. They soon faced highly inappropriate pressure from the White House to acquiesce. A lawyer for one of the funds claimed that his client was "directly threatened by the White House and in essence compelled to withdraw its opposition to the deal under threat that the full force of the White House press corps would destroy its reputation if it continued to fight."[14]

President Obama meanwhile demagogued the issue. He said of the secured creditors, "I don't stand with them. I stand with Chrysler's employees and their families and communities. I stand with Chrysler's management, its dealers, and suppliers. I stand with the millions of Americans who own and want to buy Chrysler cars. . . . It was unacceptable to let a small group of speculators endanger Chrysler's future by refusing to sacrifice like everyone else."[15] In other words, according to the president it was unacceptable to follow the law.

A few secured creditors, including the Indiana state teacher and firefighter retirement funds, ultimately sued to prevent the reorganization. Their attorneys pointed out that the sale of old Chrysler assets to new Chrysler was a sham to strip Chrysler's secured creditors of their rights. The bankruptcy court nevertheless approved the reorganization. A federal court of appeals upheld that ruling on the theory that the creditors' representative approved the reorganization on behalf of most of the secured creditors, and that approval was prudent because it allowed secured creditors to "preserve substantial value rather than risk a liquidation that might have yielded nothing at all."[16]

By the time the case reached the Supreme Court, the Court dismissed the case as moot because all of Chrysler's equity had already been distributed to the auto workers' union, the Italian carmaker Fiat (which had made a sweetheart deal with the US government), and the American and Canadian governments. But the Supreme Court also vacated the lower court opinions that had endorsed the government's extralegal bankruptcy machinations. So, while the Supreme Court had no choice but to let the government get away with what it had already done, it made sure that the lower court decisions approving the government's action could not be used as precedent in the future.[17]

The GM reorganization had its own problems, but it did not involve the same sort of shenanigans regarding secured credit holders. GM had much less secure debt, so the union funds could be bailed out without harming those creditors. The Obama administration did not publicly explain how the law allowed secured credit holders in basically the same legal position, that is, holders of Chrysler debt and holders of GM debt, to be treated so differently by government-controlled bankruptcy proceedings. The answer is that the rule of law took a backseat to expediency and political considerations.[18]

Instead of GM's secured bondholders taking the hit on behalf of Obama's union supporters, American taxpayers absorbed it instead. The US government ultimately lost $23 billion on the GM bailout. The entire loss is attributable to the Obama administration's decision to ignore bankruptcy law and exempt the auto workers' union from having to accept standard prebankruptcy concessions. The union instead received preferential treatment from Uncle Sam at the expense of everyone else.[19]

GM's dependence on the government, which held a large stake in the "new GM" postbankruptcy, led to a range of political interference by the president and Congress. This included pressure to introduce money-losing hybrid cars to promote the president's "green" agenda; pressure from the White House to close dealerships, and counterpressure from Congress (and ultimately legislation) not to; and pressure, sometimes successful, to use domestic suppliers and manufacturing facilities instead of cheaper foreign alternatives.

The Chrysler and GM bailouts were not the only examples of the Obama administration using very questionable tactics to help unions allied with the Democratic Party. Obamacare initially created tensions between labor unions and the administration. One of the labor unions' big (and entirely legitimate) selling points is that unionized workers often get generous health benefits. Various Obamacare provisions, however, threatened the viability of many health care plans unions had won for their members. Soon after Obamacare passed, the administration gave many labor unions waivers to many of these provisions.[20] In fall 2013, the Department of Health and Human Services announced that it planned to exempt some union insurance plans from a substantial new tax known as the reinsurance fee.[21]

The administration also interfered on behalf of unionized Boeing workers. In 2011, Boeing was deciding whether to locate a new production facility in Washington State or South Carolina. Boeing unions strongly preferred union-friendly Washington over South Carolina. Having been faced with costly strikes by the machinist union at its home base in Washington, Boeing told the union that the new facility would be based there only if the union accepted a long-term no-strike agreement. When the union refused, Boeing announced its intention to open the plant in South Carolina.

The National Labor Relations Board, stacked with Obama appointees, filed a legal complaint against Boeing, claiming that Boeing's request for a no-strike clause was an unfair labor practice, and that opening a plant in South Carolina was illegal retaliation for prior strikes.[22] In its response, Boeing pointed out that its contract with the machinists' union allowed the company to operate wherever it wanted without consulting the union. Also, trying to avoid labor strife is neither an unfair labor practice nor retaliation.[23]

Boeing and the machinists' union eventually reached an agreement to raise wages and expand jet production in Washington. With that done, the union no longer needed the trumped-up NLRB complaint to give it additional bargaining leverage, and it asked the board to drop the complaint. The NLRB complied. The board's acting general counsel, Lafe Solomon, admitted to the *New York Times* that its complaint against Boeing had been about helping unionized workers in Washington State, not enforcing labor law. "The case was always about the loss of future jobs in the Seattle area," he said. "This agreement has resolved that issue. There is job security in the Washington area."[24] Solomon failed to explain why it was the government's job to help workers in Washington at the expense of workers in South Carolina, or where the NLRB got the authority to tell American companies where to locate their factories.

That's not the only example of the Obama administration engaging in "extralegal intimidation," or what nonlawyers would call "illegal bullying," to get its way. Just a year and a half into the Obama administration, Judge Richard Posner, one of the nation's leading legal scholars, suggested that President Obama had already probably bullied private industry more often than any president.[25] For example, one of the first Obamacare provisions due to go into effect was apparently supposed to ban insurance companies from denying insurance to children with preexisting medical conditions. The relevant provision, however, was poorly drafted. It said that once an insurance company accepts a particular child as a customer, it could not deny the child coverage for preexisting conditions—but also suggested that the company could refuse to cover the child to begin with. The government nevertheless wrote regulations requiring coverage of children with preexisting conditions.[26]

Secretary of Health and Human Services Kathleen Sebelius sent a letter to the health insurance industry warning insurance companies to comply with the presumed original intent of the provision, and not its actual text, with an implied "or else." "Health insurance reform is designed to prevent any child from being denied coverage because he or she has a pre-existing condition," she wrote to Karen Ignagni, president of the industry trade group America's Health Insurance Plans. "Now is not the time to search for nonexistent loopholes that preserve a broken system."[27] Note the charming way in which Sebelius referred to the text of the law as a "loophole."

Normally, a trade group would either fight the imposition of a costly regulation likely not authorized by the underlying law, or at least demand substantial concessions from the government in return for compliance. The health insurance industry, however, is now so dependent on goodwill from the political powers that be that it lacks the wherewithal to fight. Instead, Ignagni immediately and meekly agreed that the industry would "fully comply."[28]

President Obama's reaction to BP's 2010 oil spill in the Gulf of Mexico was even more egregious. BP faced massive civil liability from those harmed by the spill, as well as billions of dollars in possible civil and criminal penalties. Obama, unwilling to wait for the legal process to play itself out, called a meeting with top BP executives. After undisclosed threats from Obama, the parties emerged with an agreement for BP to establish a $20 billion compensation fund. Judge Posner notes that Obama "did not pretend to have any legal authority to order this." BP also quickly complied with the president's demand that it cut its dividend to preserve cash to pay claims against it. The president going beyond his constitutional authority in this way represents, according to Posner, "a kind of 'people's democracy' regime, in which government stirs up public anger to force businesses to comply with extra-legal government demands."[29]

When not rewriting bankruptcy law, running car companies, and blackmailing big corporations, the Obama administration was undermining private property rights. Because the Supreme Court enforces only narrow constitutional protection for property, it is extremely difficult for a citizen to win, or the government to lose, a case based on property rights. It's therefore especially telling that the Obama administration managed not only to lose three property rights cases before the Supreme Court but also to lose each case 9–0, with the liberal justices unanimously rejecting the government's arguments.

The most egregious of these cases involved Michael and Chantell Sackett, a couple who owned a vacant two-thirds-acre lot in Bonner County, Idaho. Their lot is separated from the nearest body of water, Priest Lake, by several developed lots. The lot is zoned for residential use and the Sacketts tried to ensure they wouldn't have any problem building their family home on the lot. They researched permitting history and regulatory requirements, secured all required local permits, and began to build their new home. In preparing to build a house, the Sacketts filled part of their property with dirt and rock.

To the Sacketts' surprise, the federal Environmental Protection Agency decided, on legally dubious grounds, that the property contained "wetlands" that were part of Priest Lake's ecosystem. The EPA reached this decision even though the Sackett's property wasn't adjacent to any waterway and had no permanent body of water on it.

Filling the land with dirt and rock in preparation for home construction was actually, according to the EPA, illegally discharging pollutants onto wetlands. The EPA ordered the Sacketts to immediately "undertake activities to restore the site in accordance with [an EPA-created] Restoration Work Plan" and to "provide and/or obtain access to the Site" for the EPA. When the Sacketts refused to comply, they faced a fine up to $75,000 *per day*—$37,500 for violating the statute and $37,500 for violating the compliance order.

The Sacketts wanted to challenge the EPA's authority to regulate their property, but the EPA denied them a hearing. The Sacketts then went to federal court to challenge the EPA's order. The EPA responded by making the outrageous argument that the

Sacketts had no right to challenge the order within the agency, in court, or anywhere else. Rather, they had only two choices: comply with the order and shut up, or refuse to comply, wait for the EPA to bring an enforcement action for millions of dollars in fines, and challenge the enforcement action at that time.

Of course, the choices presented by the EPA were not real choices. Homeowners like the Sacketts cannot simply rack up fines that would force them into bankruptcy and hope that a court will eventually step in to save them. The EPA was really telling the Sacketts that they had to comply with the order because they had no practical way of challenging it.

Amazingly, the EPA nevertheless managed to get the Sacketts' case dismissed by a federal district court (which found that it had no jurisdiction) and to have that decision affirmed by the Ninth Circuit Court of Appeals.[30] That court found that the Clean Water Act had no provision for pre-enforcement judicial review of compliance orders, and that this did not violate the Sacketts' constitutional right not to be deprived of their liberty and property without due process of law.

Not surprisingly, the Supreme Court disagreed. The EPA, now represented by the Solicitor General's office, noted that the compliance order sent to the Sacketts was not self-executing, but required additional enforcement action by the EPA. Therefore, the government argued, the compliance order was just a step in a deliberative process rather than a coercive sanction that could be challenged.

The Court rejected this argument, and concluded instead that when the EPA denied the Sacketts' attempt to obtain a hearing, the EPA's deliberation was over. By a vote of 9–0, the Court held that the Sacketts had a right to seek review of the EPA's compliance order.[31] In Justice Samuel Alito's concurring opinion, he observed that the position taken by the federal government "would have put the property rights of ordinary Americans entirely at the mercy of EPA employees. In a nation that values due process, not to mention private property, such treatment is unthinkable."[32]

The Obama administration's second 9–0 loss in a property rights case came in *Arkansas Game & Fish Commission v. United States*.[33] The Arkansas Game & Fish Commission owns the Dave Donaldson Black River Wildlife Management Area, 23,000 acres along both banks of the Black River in Arkansas. The area supports wildlife habitats and is a hunting preserve and timber resource.

Between 1993 and 2000, the US Army Corps of Engineers periodically flooded this land. The corps released water from a dam at a slower rate than it otherwise would have to help local farmers increase harvest times. As a result, flooding increased in the spring and summer, which interfered with the commission's tree growing season. The flooding also eventually damaged the trees' root systems. When drought struck in 1999 and 2000, thousands of trees died, and more than eighteen million board feet of timber was destroyed or degraded. The trees' demise also led to the growth of other plant species in their place, making it especially expensive to restore the trees.

The commission sued the US government for compensation under the Fifth Amendment for the damage caused by the Corps of Engineers' flooding. The government responded that temporary flooding did not amount to an unconstitutional "taking" of the commission's property. After all, the property was still there, and the flooding would eventually recede. The Court of Federal Claims ruled in favor of the commission, and awarded it $5.7 million in compensation. Although the flooding was temporary, the court noted, it did permanent damage to the root systems of the trees.

The Federal Circuit Court of Appeals ruled in favor of the government.[34] The court held, implausibly, that government-induced flooding requires compensation only when the flooding is permanent or inevitably recurring; no temporary flooding caused by the government would ever require compensation. According to this logic, the government could come to your house, flood it with water, and then deny compensation for the damage because the water will eventually evaporate, the damage it caused can be fixed (at great expense), and the government *may* decide not to flood your house again.

Solicitor General Donald Verrilli, the government's top advocate, personally handled the appeal to the Supreme Court. Verrilli insisted that the government had no constitutional obligation to pay compensation for repeatedly flooding and damaging someone else's land. The Court, not surprisingly, rejected this notion, and in a 9–0 vote sent the case back to the lower courts for further consideration.[35]

The Obama administration's third 9–0 loss in property rights cases came when the United States Department of Agriculture (USDA) pursued sanctions against California raisin growers who refused to surrender a portion of their raisins to, believe it or not, a government-sponsored raisin cartel.[36] The USDA established the Raisin Administrative Committee (RAC) in 1949 to keep the prices of raisins sold in the United States high, for the benefit of raisin growers. (Your tax dollars at work!) The RAC, elected by raisin growers, decides each year how many raisins should be sold to US consumers to reach a target price for raisins.[37]

If growers grow more raisins than the target number allows for, each grower must turn over a percentage of their raisins to the RAC. The RAC, in turn, sells them abroad at a discount, or disposes of them cheaply in secondary, noncompetitive domestic markets, like school lunch programs. The growers are supposed to be reimbursed for their RAC raisins from proceeds from the sales. By 2003, however, raisin growers were forced to turn over 47 percent of their raisins to the RAC, but the RAC got so little money for them that raisin growers received no money for these raisins.[38]

Marvin and Laura Horne started producing raisins in California in 1969. After years of adhering to RAC rules, they concluded that the government's intervention in the raisin market was resulting in "grower bankruptcy, poverty, and involuntary servitude."[39] "You can't work for a whole year and then give 47 percent of what you made away and still keep that business afloat," Laura Horne said.[40]

The Hornes decided to try to evade the RAC by packing and selling their own raisins. Not having to give away almost half their raisins was good for business. Other small raisin farmers imitated the Hornes' innovation. USDA bureaucrats, however, were unwilling to let the Hornes and other small farmers leave the RAC without a fight. The USDA insisted that self-packing and sales didn't exempt the Hornes or anyone else from the RAC marketing order. The government demanded payment from the Hornes for the raisins they didn't provide to the RAC, along with hundreds of thousands of dollars in fines and penalties, adding up to over a million dollars.[41]

When the USDA filed an administrative action demanding payment, the Hornes and a few other farmers countered that the government was illegally forcing them to give away their raisins. This, they argued, constituted an unconstitutional taking of their private property without just compensation, a violation of the Fifth Amendment. An administrative law judge held the Hornes were liable for compensating the RAC and paying the fines, and declined to rule on the takings matter, as it was outside his authority.

The Hornes then raised the takings issue in federal court. The district court denied that the RAC program involved a taking of private property, while the Ninth Circuit Court of Appeals concluded that it lacked jurisdiction to consider that claim.[42] On appeal to the Supreme Court, the government argued that the Ninth Circuit was right and the Hornes' takings-based defense couldn't be heard by the court system, because the Hornes could bring a case in the Court of Federal Claims at a later date. If the Court had accepted the government's argument, it would have meant that the Hornes needed to allow their farm to be driven into bankruptcy by the fees and fines that had piled up since they stopped turning raisins over to the RAC; only then could they ask for a refund from the claims courts.

The Supreme Court disagreed, and in 2013 ruled in favor of the Hornes, allowing them to pursue the claim in federal court. The Court stated that "in the case of an administrative enforcement proceeding, when a party raises a constitutional defense to an assessed fine, it would make little sense to require the party to pay the fine in one proceeding and then turn around and sue for recovery of that same money in another proceeding."[43]

In 2015, the case returned to the Supreme Court. By an 8–1 vote, the Court held that the federal government's actions against the Hornes amounted to an illegal taking of their property. As compensation, a majority of the Court ordered that the Hornes must be released from their obligation to pay the fines and penalties they were assessed for refusing to turn over their raisins to the government.[44]

Chapter 5

"MORE CZARS THAN THE ROMANOVS"

THE GEORGE W. BUSH ADMINISTRATION was notorious for avoiding congressional oversight of high-level officials by appointing them to "czar" positions—purportedly advisory positions created by the White House, not Congress. Some of these czars had substantial legal and policy-making authority, but they were not vetted by the Senate and were not subject to Senate hearings and a vote before taking office, nor to congressional hearings and other oversight afterward.

When Senator Barack Obama was campaigning for president, he emphasized his commitment to constitutional provisions that limit the president's unilateral authority.[1] But rather than reversing the czar trend, President Obama made it worse. By May 2009, only four months after Obama's inauguration, Senator John McCain quipped that the Obama administration had "more czars than the Romanovs."[2]

Before we get to what went wrong, it's important to go over some constitutional background. Under the Constitution's Appointments Clause, "principal officers" of the United States may only be appointed with the "advice and consent" of the Senate.

This means the Senate must vote to confirm the president's high-level nominees. Over one thousand presidential appointees to important government positions require Senate confirmation. Presidential advisors, on the other hand, do not need Senate confirmation. For most of American history, the distinction was clear: appointed officials who exercise real legal authority are subject to the Appointments Clause, mere advisors are not.

This distinction between high-level advisors and principal officers is often lost in discussions of presidential czars. This chapter limits its definition of "czar" to an individual who is not confirmed by the Senate and exercises final decision-making authority. A czar actually dictates or controls policy or the enforcement of laws and regulations. This may include controlling budgetary programs, administering or coordinating a policy area, or otherwise making or enforcing binding rules and regulations.[3] It is these "czars," and not mere advisors (no matter how influential), whose positions violate the Constitution.

Czars were not much of a problem until the George W. Bush administration. In the early twentieth century, Presidents Woodrow Wilson and Franklin Roosevelt each neglected to get Senate approval for purported advisors who had real authority. But even these powerful wartime presidents used czars only infrequently, and they failed to set a firm precedent.[4] Indeed, as late as the 1970s, Presidents Ford and Carter had no czars, President Reagan had three czars, and Presidents George H. W. Bush and Clinton had two each.[5] These occasional czars were hardly ideal as a constitutional matter, but they didn't exactly create a constitutional crisis, either.

President George W. Bush caused a much larger constitutional breach when he created eight czar positions, which were filled by eleven different individuals. Bush's appointment of Tom Ridge as homeland security czar after 9/11 brazenly defied the normal appointments process. Bush appointed Ridge three weeks before he even issued an executive order creating the office.

After the trauma of 9/11, the Republican-controlled Congress would have created virtually any homeland security office and confirmed virtually any officer the president asked for. The administration nevertheless chose to portray Ridge as a mere advisor to evade congressional oversight. The White House ordered Ridge to refuse to testify before Congress, to promote the idea that he was only a presidential advisor. Democratic Senator Robert Byrd and Republican Senator Ted Stevens objected that Ridge was the single most important federal official working to improve homeland security, and Congress needed to hear from him.[6] The White House did not budge.

Eventually, Congress preempted Ridge's office by creating a real executive department subject to oversight, the Department of Homeland Security, over Bush's initial opposition. Bush eventually realized that Ridge would be more effective if members of Congress weren't constantly trying to stifle his efforts due to a lack of congressional oversight, so Bush appointed Ridge to be the first Secretary of Homeland Security.

Bush's use of czars, along with other Bush administration policies concentrating power in the president, created a backlash Barack Obama rode when he ran for president. Obama was expected to limit or even eliminate the use of czars. Instead, he substantially expanded the role of czars, creating a total of twenty czar positions in his first term, or over twice as many as Bush had created in two terms.

President Obama's apologists later argued that he was forced to resort to czars due to the Senate's reluctance to confirm his appointees. That's false. Obama started using czars during the early "honeymoon" phase of his presidency, when the Democrats had a filibuster-proof Senate majority. At that time, he surely could have found many qualified nominees that the Senate would have easily and quickly confirmed.

In late 2008, the incoming Obama administration announced that Clinton administration Environmental Protection Agency administrator Carol Browner would serve as "Assistant to the President for Energy and Climate Change," popularly known as the "Energy Czar" or "climate czar." Browner was not appointed to a position requiring confirmation because President Obama knew she would have had a very difficult confirmation process. First, in the Clinton administration she had been a strong advocate of controversial positions opposed by senators from both parties. More important, she ordered all of her files, and those of other top EPA officials, destroyed on her last day in office—the same day that a federal judge issued an order requiring her to preserve those files because of ongoing litigation. The judge ultimately held the EPA in contempt of court for its "contumacious conduct."[7]

Because Browner officially was only an advisor to President Obama, she had no confirmation hearings, and she refused to testify before Congress to assist with its routine oversight duties. But Browner was an advisor in title only; her responsibilities and influence in the Obama administration were "vastly greater" than those of Obama's EPA administrator, Lisa Jackson.[8] Among other things, Browner was the individual most responsible for the Obama administration's climate change initiatives.

Obama also appointed a green jobs czar named Van Jones. Jones's official title was "Council on Environmental Quality's Special Advisor on Green Jobs." Jones had a long history of involvement with a variety of far-left and black nationalist groups. He had to resign after controversial statements by him surfaced. First, he told an audience in February 2009, just before he joined the administration, that congressional Republicans were "assholes." Next, a blogger revealed that Jones had signed a petition in 2004 that called for an investigation into whether "people within the [Bush] administration may indeed have deliberately allowed 9/11 to happen, perhaps as a pretext for war." The Obama administration suggested that Jones had not read the petition carefully, and Jones claimed that the petition "does not reflect my views now or ever."[9]

Conservative websites, smelling blood, then reveled in describing the various extremist and kooky groups that Jones had recently belonged to, and, in some cases, founded.[10] The Obama administration cut its losses and forced Jones to resign. Republican critics pointed out that if Jones had been vetted via the confirmation process, his dubious background and affiliations would have come to light, saving the president some embarrassment and the country Van Jones.[11]

President Obama also created the Office of Urban Affairs by executive order in February 2009. The director of this office was a czar not subject to Senate confirmation. The director was given authority "to coordinate the development of the policy agenda for urban America across executive departments and agencies," "to coordinate all aspects of urban policy," and to target federal expenditures.[12]

Meanwhile, White House chef Sam Kass was named to the positions of food initiative coordinator and senior policy advisor for healthy food initiatives, while retaining his position as chef. He was not subject to Senate confirmation even though he was given authority to coordinate policy for a $400 million initiative. Kass is also a longtime friend of the Obama family, making the whole arrangement suspicious—at the very least the sort of thing that the Senate would have looked into had it been given the opportunity to hold confirmation hearings.[13]

In March 2009, Obama named Nancy-Ann DeParle to run the White House Office of Health Reform. Her position became known as the health reform czar. Even though she was officially just an advisor, DeParle was given substantial policy responsibilities, including coordinating the Obama administration's health care reform efforts.[14] Her job therefore overlapped substantially with that of the Secretary of Health and Human Services. Unlike

DeParle, the HHS Secretary had actual legal authority over health care issues and had been confirmed to her position by the Senate.

In March 2009, the president appointed an auto industry recovery czar, Ed Montgomery, with the formal title of "Director of Recovery for Auto Communities and Workers." Montgomery had the authority to distribute billions of dollars to "help lift up the hardest-hit areas by using the unprecedented levels of funding available in our Recovery Act." In June of that year, the president established a new White House Council on Automotive Communities and Workers, directed and coordinated by the auto recovery czar.[15]

Montgomery was not subject to confirmation because he was supposedly just an advisor, yet he was given authority for distributing huge amounts of money and coordinating policy within the entire executive branch. Montgomery resigned in 2010, and was replaced with two officials, Secretary of Labor Hilda Solis and National Economic Council director Larry Summers (who was never confirmed by the Senate to the latter nonadvisory "advisory" position), again without any input from Congress.[16]

As previously mentioned, Obama also had a separate "car czar" who served as the chief advisor to the Presidential Task Force on the Auto Industry. Steven Rattner, the first car czar, was never subject to Senate confirmation nor to congressional oversight. The source of Rattner's authority was supposed to be the Troubled Asset Relief Program passed by Congress as part of the Emergency Economic Stabilization Act of 2008. But TARP provided for the bailout of financial institutions, not car companies, and the extension of TARP to auto companies was essentially lawless. TARP certainly did not provide for the appointment of an unconfirmed car czar to run two of America's largest companies, Chrysler and General Motors. Rattner exerted huge influence on the auto industry in the six months he held the car czar position, and later bragged that he succeeded because he "didn't have to deal with Congress."[17] (For more on TARP shenanigans, see chapter 4.)

Rattner's replacement as car czar in July 2009, Ron Bloom, formerly of the United Steelworkers, was equally immune from congressional and public oversight. If nothing else, it would have been interesting to see how Bloom would have explained at a confirmation hearing the following remarks he made in 2008: "Generally speaking, we get the joke. We know that the free market is nonsense. We know that the whole point is to game the system, to beat the market. Or at least find someone who will pay you a lot of money, 'cause they're convinced that there is a free lunch. We know this is largely about power, that it's an adults-only, no-limit game. We kind of agree with Mao, that political power comes largely from the barrel of a gun."[18]

Early in the Obama administration, some Democratic senators joined their Republican counterparts in questioning the constitutionality of Obama's promiscuous delegation of legal and policy-making authority to unconfirmed czars not subject to Senate oversight. These Democrats included Dianne Feinstein, Byron Dorgan, Russell Feingold, and Robert Byrd. Feinstein, for example, suggested that unconfirmed czar positions were a "problem" and that more oversight of the officers involved was needed. Feingold wrote a letter to the president objecting to his appointment of czars.[19] And Byrd pointed out that "the rapid and easy accumulation of power by White House staff can threaten the constitutional system of checks and balances. At the worst, White House staff have taken direction and control of programmatic areas that are the statutory responsibility of Senate-confirmed officials."[20]

White House counsel Gregory Craig replied to Feinstein, but dishonestly. As Sollenberger and Rozell explain, "he cherry picked certain offices to characterize allegations of too many czars as being overstated as false. He maneuvers around questions about accountability by saying that staff of departments and agencies can testify, or that maybe certain czars can do so. And he inaccurately labels some figures with substantial policy and spending authority as possessing no more than an advisory role within the White House."[21]

The Obama administration found that many of its czars were less effective than its confirmed appointees, so Obama's enthusiasm for appointing czars waned.[22] That enthusiasm diminished further when, after the 2010 elections, Republican Congressman Darrell Issa, who would soon take over as chair of the House Committee on Oversight and Government Reform, promised to investigate the "unconfirmed czars," a potent symbol of the "arrogance of government."[23]

This was too late to preempt Obama's most egregious appointment of a czar. He appointed controversial Harvard Law School professor (and future Massachusetts senator) Elizabeth Warren assistant to the president to oversee the creation of a new consumer financial protection bureau in 2010. The president knew that Warren faced a tough confirmation fight, so he invented a phony "advisory" position for her that didn't require confirmation. Warren's job description was to lead a team of three dozen or so individuals to get the new Consumer Financial Protection Bureau up and running. As liberal Yale Law School professor Bruce Ackerman pointed out, Warren was to be a "key executive" in the Treasury Department and therefore, Ackerman wrote, should like other key officials be "required to run the gauntlet of Senate approval." Instead, Ackerman concluded, Warren's appointment marked "another milestone down the path toward an imperial presidency."[24]

Meanwhile, the US Chamber of Commerce fumed, "By not allowing Ms. Warren's nomination to be considered through the regular order of the full Senate confirmation process, the administration has circumvented one of the very few checks on a big new agency that already has been given an unprecedented concentration of regulatory power. This maneuver is an affront to the pledge of transparency and consumer protection that's purported to be the focus of this new agency." Even the left-wing advocacy group Public Citizen expressed disappointment that President Obama failed to formally nominate Warren (or anyone else) to run the new bureau. "Warren is confirmable, and a fight over her confirmation is worth having," a spokesman said.[25]

On the other hand, Massachusetts Democratic Congressman Barney Frank congratulated "the administration on its creativity," with creativity in this context apparently meaning "ability to sidestep the Constitution to achieve partisan goals."[26] A White House official told the New York Times that "Mr. Obama and Ms. Warren both felt it was better to get her started on establishing an agency from scratch than on getting mired in a long confirmation fight or a controversy over a recess appointment."[27] Why, after all, let the Constitution get in the way of "establishing an agency"?

Congress, at the Republicans' insistence, took a step to curb Obama's use of czars in a 2011 budget compromise bill. Section 2262 of the bill barred spending money on four named White House "czar" positions.[28] President Obama signed the bill into law, but also issued a statement suggesting that section 2262 was an unconstitutional infringement on the president's constitutional powers, and that he intended to enforce the law in a way that would preserve his authority. This statement conflicted with the president's campaign promise that he would not use signing statements to evade a statute.

For example, at one campaign appearance, a citizen asked him, "Do you promise not to use presidential signing statements to get your way?" Obama responded "yes." And then, after a lengthy critique of George W. Bush's attempt to "accumulate more power in the presidency," Obama firmly promised, "We're not gonna use signing statements as a way of doing an end-run around Congress."[29]

To understand the salience of Obama's remark, we need to briefly review the history of the controversy over presidential signing statements. The Reagan administration was the first to use signing statements regularly. Congress, administration lawyers felt, had been abusing legislative history. It passed ambiguous legislation but then created official legislative history after the fact to influence how courts would interpret the law. Reagan's signing statements were meant to give the president a similar opportunity to influence judges by explaining the executive branch's understanding of the law.[30]

The George H. W. Bush administration used signing statement for a different reason: to contest the constitutionality of certain provisions of the very law the president was signing. Unlike many governors, the president has no authority to veto individual provisions of a large bill (the so-called line item veto.) The Constitution provides the president with only two basic options when presented with a bill passed by Congress—he can sign the entire bill or veto it. Under normal circumstances, the president would have the duty to veto an unconstitutional bill.

The modern legislative process, however, has created a problem. Congress increasingly sends the president omnibus legislation to sign that has items dealing with dozens, hundreds, or even thousands of different matters.[31] These bills often contain provisions that are critical to the functioning of government—paying for new weaponry for soldiers at war, paying government employee salaries, and the like. Bush therefore decided to sign such bills into law, but reserved the right to refuse to enforce individual provisions that he deemed unconstitutional.

The Clinton administration continued the Bush administration's practice of issuing signing statements objecting to unconstitutional provisions of bills signed by the president. Following the advice of OLC head Walter Dellinger, Clinton limited his objections in signing statements to what he saw as unconstitutional encroachments on executive (i.e., presidential) power.[32] For example, Clinton signed a law that among other things prohibited the president from transferring military equipment to the United Nations without fifteen days' notice to Congress. The president issued a signing statement stating that he would not abide by that provision because it interfered with his powers as commander-in-chief.[33] Meanwhile, the Clinton administration continued to enforce other unconstitutional provisions of large bills when those provisions did not impinge on executive power.

The Dellinger rule is exactly backward. The last place that a president should exercise any authority he may have to refuse to enforce a section of a bill he has signed is when it conflicts with the president's self-interest in a broad definition of executive power. If the president wants to preserve his prerogatives, that's exactly when the president should use political capital to threaten to veto a law that will encroach on his power and, if that threat isn't effective, to go ahead and veto the bill. When the president is not self-interested, that is, when a provision does not impinge on his own power, the president should have significantly more authority to refuse to enforce unconstitutional provisions of a very broad and long bill that Congress sends him.

Despite all this, until President George W. Bush came into office, signing statements were only a minor blip on the constitutional radar, as presidents used them sparingly. Bush, however, used signing statements to challenge the constitutionality of provisions of bills signed into law more often than had all previous presidents combined. He also used his veto power less than almost any president.[34] Critics pointed out that the Bush administration seemed to use signing statements as a first, rather than last, resort, upsetting the balance of power between Congress and the president by allowing the president, in effect, to amend legislation as he signed it.

Even many Republican and conservative lawyers were highly

uncomfortable with the way the Bush administration consistently refused to enforce statutory restraint on executive power. They suggested that President Bush was acting as a judge in his own case, and always ruling in his own favor.[35] Northwestern University law professor Steven Calabresi, for example, a founder of the conservative Federalist Society, argued that the president should only refuse to enforce laws that are clearly unconstitutional and only when confronted with existing legislation. Otherwise, the president is obligated to either veto a bill or enforce all of its provisions. Calabresi allowed for an exception when true exigencies prevented the president from vetoing particular legislation.[36]

The American Bar Association also weighed in, issuing a report signed by both liberal and conservative lawyers and law professors condemning the use of signing statements.[37] The ABA argued that the president's only remedy if he thinks a provision of a bill is unconstitutional is to veto the entire bill. Unlike a signing statement, a veto can be overruled by Congress via a two-thirds vote, giving Congress the final say, rather than giving the president an extraconstitutional power to invalidate legislation.

Presidents, however, are understandably reluctant to hold the government hostage to relatively minor unconstitutional provisions that they can instead simply refuse to enforce. And some legal scholars argue that presidents should sign massive bills containing constitutionally dubious provisions, and wait for those provisions to be challenged in court by private plaintiffs. The problem with that idea is that often there is no private plaintiff who has "standing," that is, the legal right, to challenge a particular provision in court.[38]

The signing statements issue became sufficiently politically "hot" during the waning years of the Bush administration that, as we have seen, Obama promised on the campaign trail not to use them to circumvent Congress. This was not an off-the-cuff gaffe; in December 2007, Obama, responding in writing to a

Boston Globe questionnaire, promised that "I will not use signing statements to nullify or undermine congressional instructions as enacted into law."[39]

To say the least, these statements and promises were inconsistent with Obama's signing statement objecting to section 2262, barring the use of federal funds for certain czar positions. Nor was the content of the objections persuasive. First, Obama claimed that a president "has well-established authority to supervise and oversee the executive branch, and to obtain advice in furtherance of this supervisory authority." In fact, Congress has the authority to reshape any part of the executive branch; the president only has supervisory authority over what Congress gives him.[40]

Obama also claimed "the prerogative to obtain advice," including from advisors within the White House. The president may, in fact, seek advice from anyone he wants to, but "the President has no open-ended authority that is not subject to democratic controls to hire whomever he pleases and have the public pay their salaries."[41] Given that Congress can create executive branch positions, it can also eliminate positions, including positions that a president establishes on his own authority.[42] As a leading expert on the subject, Fordham Law School's Aaron Saiger, puts it, Obama's argument that Congress has "a constitutional duty to fund a presidential staff as large as the President might desire" is not just wrong, it's "frivolous."[43]

President Obama also claimed that section 2262 violated the separation of powers "by undermining the President's ability to exercise his constitutional responsibilities and take care that the laws be faithfully executed." In fact, however, Obama's czars were doing jobs allocated by statute to others, including confirmed cabinet secretaries. Congress was trying not to degrade the president's ability to enforce the law, but to prevent the president from evading congressional oversight of high-level government officials. As Sollenberger and Rozell put it, Obama's signing statement showed "utter contempt for Congress as a coequal branch of government."[44]

In the end, however, the president decided to avoid a constitutional confrontation over section 2262 (though he did resort to additional Bush-like signing statements in the future).[45] Instead of funding the positions that Congress had officially defunded, the president simply renamed the relevant positions. This was possible because Congress had enumerated the positions to be eliminated by title rather than by responsibilities. For example, while the law banned the president from spending money on an Assistant to the President for Energy and Climate Change, the relevant individual's position became *Deputy* Assistant to the President for Energy and Climate Change. So the Obama administration was able to obey the letter, but not the spirit, of the law—but only after issuing a signing statement directly violating the president's own claimed understanding of his constitutional responsibilities.

The ultimate underlying rationale for having "czars" is that it creates efficiency in government—the president can appoint whomever he wants, free from confirmation hearings and votes. And then the czar can do whatever he wants, without meaningful congressional oversight. This may, in fact, be more efficient than the system set up by the Constitution, although Saiger argues that Obama's czar system "reenacts, rather than counteracts, pathologies associated with interagency coordination, overlap, and conflict."[46]

Indeed, Obama's czars clashed with cabinet officials whose portfolios overlapped with the czars'. By March 2011, Obama's new chief of staff, William M. Daley, had to repair badly frayed relations between the president and his cabinet. Part of the problem, according to the *Washington Post*, was the plethora of czars who often got more attention from the president than did his cabinet secretaries. "The White House loops people out. The czars keep people from getting in," one senior Democratic official remarked.[47]

It's impossible to know what, if anything, Obama's czars accomplished to make up for the problems they caused and the disrespect for the rule of law they embodied. As one critic notes, "they don't report to anybody. . . . They don't testify before Congress. They don't publish. We don't know how many personnel are involved, or who they might be. We don't know how much has been spent by them, and on what. We don't know, to paraphrase Donald Rumsfeld, what we don't know."[48]

Regardless, the Constitution was built for deliberation, not for speed. The Founding Fathers sought to create a system of checks and balances that prevents any branch of government from becoming tyrannical. The rise of the czars threatens that goal. Hopefully, the political problems the czars caused President Obama mean that the American czar system will share the fate of the Russian one.

Chapter 6

OBAMACARE ABOVE ALL

THE AFFORDABLE CARE ACT, popularly known as Obamacare, has been a constitutional and rule-of-law disaster. The problems with Obamacare can be divided into three categories: (1) the reckless, dishonest, and grossly irresponsible way the Democrats promoted and passed Obamacare; (2) important Obamacare provisions that range from constitutionally dubious to blatantly unconstitutional; and (3) the illegal ways the Obama administration has delayed, ignored, and modified various Obamacare provisions to suit its political agenda.

President Obama made passing a major bill reforming American health care his top priority. One problem he faced is that no congressional Republicans were willing to sign on to Obamacare. Democrats blamed this on the Republicans' desire to be obstructionist. Republicans retorted that the Democrats never seriously sought their input. Rather, they tried to pay just enough lip service to Republicans to entice a few of them to give the Democrats' health care bill a bipartisan veneer.

Regardless, in the past a lack of bipartisan buy-in would have been sufficient to kill any dreams of a wholesale health care reform. No major social initiative in over one hundred years had passed Congress without support from both sides of the aisle—

for example, Social Security, Medicare and Medicaid, and the Civil Rights Act of 1964 and other major antidiscrimination initiatives all received broad bipartisan support.[1] Such bipartisanship was crucial to the long-term success of these laws. It meant that both parties had a stake in them, and that the laws reflected widespread public support.

By contrast, Obamacare's failure to attract any Republican support reflected the fact that it never received majority support in public opinion polls, and that those Americans who knew the most about it were most likely to be opposed. The Obama administration dismissed such opposition as temporary. After all, the public was dissatisfied with the existing health care system, and after the 2008 elections the Democrats had a significant majority in the House as well as a sixty-vote, filibuster-proof majority in the Senate. Obama and his allies were convinced that their health care reforms would ultimately prove popular, and would help the Democrats cement their emerging national majority for decades to come.

But first they had to pass a law. When he ran for president, Obama, in contrast to his primary opponent Hillary Clinton, pledged to oppose a requirement that uninsured individuals purchase health insurance, a requirement that came to be known as the individual mandate. Health economists warned, however, that for Obamacare to work, it had to mandate that young, healthy people vastly overpay for health insurance compared to their anticipated health care needs. The young healthys would cross-subsidize the sicker, older Americans who would be eligible for health insurance at a price well below the expected costs to insure them.

Obama therefore reluctantly agreed to include a provision in Obamacare that required all Americans to either have health insurance or pay a penalty to the government. Because the president had vowed not to raise taxes on the middle class, Democrats from President Obama on down insisted that the penalty for not having health insurance was just that, and was not a tax.[2]

To neutralize the organized opposition that had killed the Clinton administration's health care efforts, the Obama administration negotiated with the pharmaceutical industry, representatives of American doctors, lobby groups for the elderly, the hospital industry, and other major constituencies. Each received assurances that their interests would be taken care of, and each was sufficiently appeased that it agreed not to oppose the president's plan.

To dampen public opposition, President Obama and his allies knowingly and repeatedly lied about how the pending legislation would work once implemented. Most notoriously, the president publicly claimed dozens of times that Obamacare would allow those who liked their current health care plans to keep them. Each time, it was a blatant lie.[3]

The Democratic leadership, fearful that momentum for Obamacare was fading as it continued to poll poorly, decided to rush a bill through the Senate before Christmas 2009. On November 18, Majority Leader Harry Reid merged two separate pending bills into a bill to be voted on by the Senate. To shore up support among wavering Democratic senators, Reid provided expensive special favors for their states, most notoriously the "Louisiana Purchase" to win Senator Mary Landrieu's vote, and the "Cornhusker Kickback" to win Nebraska Senator Ben Nelson's.

The Senate bill also had to overcome a constitutional barrier. It contained several new taxes, and the Constitution mandates that all revenue-raising bills originate in the House, not the Senate. To try to evade that requirement, the Senate took a completely unrelated bill, the "Service Members Home Ownership Tax Act of 2009," that had passed the House months earlier, stripped out all of its existing language, and replaced it with the language of the Senate bill. The Senate Democrats then claimed that this meant that for constitutional purposes the Senate bill originated in the House. The Supreme Court may ultimately decide if this maneuver met constitutional requirements, but meanwhile it underscores the extent to which the Senate Democrats were willing to at least bend constitutional rules to get Obamacare passed.

To meet the self-imposed Christmas deadline, Reid provided only six days for debate on the final version of the bill. The Senate bill passed on a strict party line vote, 60–39. Few people, including senators and their staffs, had time to read the whole 2,700-page bill, much less note any possible weaknesses, flaws, or ambiguities. Reid and other Senate Democrats weren't terribly worried about this. The bill was set to go to the House, then back to the Senate, then to "reconciliation" between the House and the Senate versions, and then to the president for his signature. Everyone thought there would be plenty of opportunities to make changes.

But a major impediment arose soon after the Senate bill passed. Democratic Senator Ted Kennedy had died that past summer, and the January special election to replace him was won by Republican Scott Brown, who ran as a strong opponent of Obamacare. This deprived the Democrats of their filibuster-proof majority in the Senate, and meant that the Senate would not be able to pass a revised bill. The only way to pass Obamacare at this point was to have the House vote on legislation identical to the Senate bill, while engaging in legally dubious procedural maneuvering. And that's what the Democrats did.

The House passed the Senate bill as-is, and then also passed a separate reconciliation bill with minor changes, eliminating some of the law's most egregious features, including the Cornhusker Kickback. The president then signed the original House/Senate bill. Once he did that, the Senate took up the reconciliation bill, which, unlike ordinary legislation subject to filibuster, could be passed by a simple majority vote. It was highly unusual, though not entirely unheard of, for Congress to evade the filibuster via the reconciliation process.

To recap, to pass Obamacare, President Obama and congressional Democrats acted over the opposition of public opinion and of every single congressional Republican. President Obama broke a firm campaign promise to oppose requiring individuals to purchase health insurance, bought off major interest groups, and lied repeatedly in asserting that those who liked their current health care plans could keep them. After Senate Majority Leader Harry Reid bribed reluctant senators with goodies for their respective states, Congress ultimately passed a Senate bill that nobody wanted, and, indeed, that likely no one had read in its entirety when the Senate passed it, and that certainly no one fully understood. Senator Max Baucus, one of Obamacare's chief architects, not only acknowledged not reading the bill, but opined that it would have been a "waste of time" to do so, because only experts could understand it.[4] As House Majority Leader Nancy Pelosi infamously remarked, Congress had to pass the bill to find out what was in it. To evade its constitutional responsibilities, the Senate pretended that its bill actually originated in the House, and Congress used an extraordinary procedural maneuver to allow the House to make some politically expedient amendments to the law and evade a filibuster.

Otto von Bismarck remarked that laws are like sausages—it's better not to see how they are made. If Obamacare represents how American law is made, especially a law that reorganized almost twenty percent of the American economy, surely the congressional sausage factory should be condemned by public health authorities.

Obama and the Democrats, however, believed that two things would happen that would justify their actions. First, Obamacare would become increasingly popular, and, second, that the Democrats would continue to control both houses of Congress. Obama and congressional Democrats therefore assumed that any sna-fus that arose because Obamacare consisted of a hastily drafted Senate bill never meant to become law could be easily fixed by Congress.

Meanwhile, once enacted, Obamacare faced a significant constitutional hurdle: the apparent absence of constitutional authority for the federal government to require individuals to buy health insurance. Article I, Section 8 of the Constitution lists a wide range of powers given to Congress, including setting bankruptcy and intellectual property laws, raising a military, establishing the post office, coining money, and so on.

Congress's most capacious power, however, has turned out to be its power to regulate "commerce among the states" under Article I, Section 8's Commerce Clause. As the federal government consistently grew after the Civil War, so did the Supreme Court's interpretation of Congress's power to regulate interstate commerce. By the 1940s, the Supreme Court held that Congress had the power to regulate a farmer who sought to grow wheat on his land to feed his own family and livestock. The Court reasoned that if a lot of farmers evaded federal production quotas by taking their wheat out of the commercial market, it would in the aggregate have a "substantial effect" on interstate commerce. And even if such activity was not likely to have a substantial effect on interstate commerce, it was sufficient that Congress had a rational basis for thinking it might.[5]

Since then, it has been an article of faith among liberals that the power to regulate commerce among the states essentially allows the federal government to do anything not forbidden by the Bill of Rights. They reason that in our modern interconnected world, almost any activity, considered in the aggregate, may affect interstate commerce.

Conservative and libertarian legal scholars have almost universally rejected this interpretation of the commerce power.

First, they note that such an interpretation of Congress's power is contrary to the original meaning of the Commerce Clause. Second, they point out that if the Commerce Clause gave Congress the authority to regulate everything, there was no reason for the Constitution to enumerate Congress's other powers. While right-leaning legal scholars disagree on the extent to which the Court's existing Commerce Clause precedents should be reversed, they agree that these precedents were mistaken, and certainly should not be expanded.[6]

For almost sixty years, no law was successfully challenged as beyond Congress's commerce power. But in 1995 and again in 2000, a five-justice conservative Supreme Court majority invalidated federal laws as being outside Congress's regulatory authority. The Court insisted that the power be limited to regulating commercial activity and not, those decisions held, to merely possessing a gun in a school zone or engaging in domestic violence.[7] Many liberal constitutional scholars panicked, worried that the Court was poised to take the Constitution back to what President Franklin Roosevelt derisively called the horse-and-buggy days when the federal government was one of limited and enumerated powers.[8]

A Supreme Court decision in 2005, however, rejected a Commerce Clause challenge to a federal ban on the growing and consumption of home-grown marijuana for personal, medicinal purposes.[9] Progressives persuaded themselves that this meant that the 1995 and 2000 opinions could be dismissed as mere symbolic anomalies. Two of the three dissenters in the marijuana case, Justices William Rehnquist and Sandra Day O'Connor, soon retired. It seemed as if the constitutional coast was clear for Congress to do whatever it wanted.

The Supreme Court, in fact, had never given carte blanche to Congress to abuse its commerce power. Rather, the Court's decisions emphasized that it was deferring to Congress's conclusion that its laws were within the commerce power. Congress, therefore, had the responsibility to police itself. But Congress has long since ceased to be a body that engaged in serious constitutional debate or reflection. Congress instead relied on the Supreme Court to deal with any constitutional objections to its laws. Democrats therefore spent little energy considering whether Obamacare's mandate that Americans buy health insurance was within Congress's power.

On the other side of the political spectrum, since the 1990s conservative and libertarian constitutionalists had grown increasingly interested in limiting Congress to its enumerated powers. When Obamacare was under consideration, Tea Party activists challenged various Democratic senators and representatives to explain the constitutional source of Congress's authority to require the purchase of health insurance. House Speaker Nancy Pelosi, reflecting the ingrained progressive view that Congress's power was unlimited and therefore its exercise need not be justified, famously replied with a mocking, "Are you serious? Are you serious?"

Other Democratic congressmen responded to the Tea Partiers with equal perspicacity:

■ Representative John Conyers cited the "Good and Welfare Clause" as the source of Congress's authority (there is no such clause);

■ Representative Peter Stark responded, "The federal government can do most anything in this country";

■ Representative Phil Hare said, "I don't worry about the Constitution on this, to be honest. . . . It doesn't matter to me";

■ Senator Daniel Akaka said he was "not aware" of which Constitutional provision authorizes the healthcare bill; and

- Senator Patrick Leahy added, "We have plenty of authority. Are you saying there's no authority?"

Perhaps the most telling answer came from Representative James Clyburn, who opined, "There's nothing in the Constitution that says the federal government has anything to do with most of the stuff we do. How about [you] show me where in the Constitution it prohibits the federal government from doing this?"[10]

Conservative and libertarian legal scholars rightly suspected that congressional Democrats' cavalier attitude toward the doctrine of enumerated powers provided an opening to challenge the constitutionality of Obamacare. Led by Georgetown University Center law professor Randy Barnett, they crafted a clever challenge to the individual mandate's constitutionality—no matter how broad Congress's power to regulate commercial *activity*, they argued, the Constitution does not give Congress the power to regulate *inactivity*, i.e., the failure to purchase health insurance. They added that Congress had never before used its commerce power to require individuals to purchase a commercial product. This meant that Obamacare was an unprecedented power grab by Congress, one never endorsed by even the most expansive prior Supreme Court rulings on the commerce power.[11]

As plaintiffs, including many states represented by their attorneys general, lined up to challenge Obamacare in court, the law's defenders used a combination of bravado and derision to try to stunt the challenges. Obamacare's defenders claimed that the law was obviously constitutional, that the Supreme Court was likely to rule 9–0 or 8–1 in favor of the government, and that any arguments that the law ran afoul of the Commerce Clause were ridiculous, made up by ideologues solely to bring down Obamacare.

In fact, not only had right-leaning jurists long objected to turning the Commerce Clause into an "Everything Clause" but also specific doubts about the constitutionality of a federal requirement to purchase health insurance had been raised in the early 1990s when the Clinton health care plan was being debated.[12] President Obama himself privately expressed concern in 2009 that if Obamacare included an individual mandate it would be vulnerable to constitutional challenge.[13]

When the litigation reached the Supreme Court, sophisticated liberal lawyers who were closely following the Obamacare litigation begged Solicitor General Donald Verrilli to identify a limiting principle that would allow the Court to uphold Obamacare while not giving Congress the power to regulate anything it wanted.[14] Verrilli, however, was apparently unable to fathom that conservatives demurred from the liberal consensus that the commerce power was limitless. Not only did he decline to identify a limiting principle in his brief to the Supreme Court but also, when Justices Alito, Kennedy, and Scalia asked him at oral argument to identify a limiting principle, the experienced, normally silver-tongued Verrilli became incoherent.[15]

Not only did Verrilli's argument on the Commerce Clause issue go poorly but also a majority of justices seemed to sympathize with another constitutional challenge to Obamacare, that it was unconstitutional for the law to condition all federal funding for Medicaid on the states agreeing to Obamacare's vast expansion of that program.[16] Deprivation of federal Medicaid funding would result in bankruptcy for most states, making state participation in Obamacare's Medicaid expansion a "your money or your life" type of choice. Past precedents had suggested that coercing the states in this manner might be unconstitutional, though the exact contours of that prohibition were unclear.

After the Obamacare case was argued before the Supreme Court, word apparently leaked that the preliminary vote by the justices was 5–4 to invalidate all of Obamacare as beyond Congress's commerce power.[17] The Obama administration and its allies, growing increasingly concerned that they were going to lose the case, unleashed a campaign of preemptive vilification against the five conservatives on the Court in general and on Chief Justice John Roberts in particular.[18] President Obama, breaking a norm that presidents don't comment on pending Supreme Court cases lest they be seen as trying to illegitimately influence the Court's deliberations, led the charge.[19]

Chief Justice Roberts ultimately switched sides and voted to mostly uphold Obamacare, giving the administration a 5–4 victory.[20] Why Roberts did so, and to what extent it was a response to the intense public pressure pro-Obamacare forces put on him, with threats to delegitimize the Supreme Court if it voted the "wrong" way, remains a matter of speculation.

Roberts joined the other four conservatives in concluding that Congress lacked the power under the Commerce Clause to require individuals to buy health insurance. Roberts then proceeded to uphold the individual mandate on the theory that it could be interpreted to be not a penalty, but a tax on those who failed to buy health insurance. As a tax, Roberts voted to uphold the individual mandate as within Congress's constitutional authority to lay taxes for the general welfare.[21]

Roberts reached this conclusion even though the Obama administration and congressional Democrats had sworn up and down that the individual mandate was not a tax, even though Roberts acknowledged that the individual mandate was not a tax for the purposes of a law called the Anti-Injunction Act, even though the individual mandate was not located in the revenue section of the law, even though according to Roberts himself it was not a tax per the "most straightforward" or "most natural" reading of the law, and even though the individual mandate does not seem to fit into any of the categories of federal tax permitted by the Constitution.[22] Roberts nevertheless concluded, as one critic put it, that the penalty could be deemed "a tax for constitutional purposes if he squinted hard enough, used his imagination, and climbed through Alice's rabbit hole."[23]

Roberts pulled an even more egregious sleight of hand when upholding Obamacare's Medicaid expansion. Four justices voted to hold the expansion entirely unconstitutional, and to invalidate the rest of Obamacare as dependent on the unconstitutional expansion. Roberts, along with two of the more liberal justices, agreed that conditioning all Medicaid funds on states' expanding Medicaid eligibility was coercive and therefore unconstitutional. But instead of voting to invalidate the law, Roberts rewrote the Medicaid statute to separate "Old Medicaid," i.e., what existed before Obamacare, and "New Medicaid," i.e., the Medicaid expansion. He allowed the government to condition New Medicaid funding on agreeing to the Medicaid expansion, but banned the federal government from denying Old Medicaid funds to states that refused the expansion.[24]

Nothing in the text of the law allowed, or even hinted at, the Court's ability to divide Medicaid into two separate entities, but Roberts did it anyway to save Obamacare. Once again, we can only speculate as to Roberts's motives. Whatever motivated him, however, was not a fair reading of the text of the underlying statute.

Another major constitutional challenge to Obamacare will likely arise in 2017. Achieving Obamacare's goal of controlling Medicare costs depends heavily on something called the Independent Payment Advisory Board. The IPAB will be composed of up to fifteen appointed experts who, starting in 2017, will get to cut Medicare spending without going through anything resembling a normal administrative process, and without the consent of Congress or the president. Congress may preempt the IPAB's cuts with cuts of its own, but Obamacare requires a majority in the House, a three-fifths vote in the Senate, and the president's signature to enact any replacement legislation that spends more than the board's proposal.

Obamacare also purports to forbid the IPAB from being dissolved absent a three-fifths vote of both houses of Congress, along with the president's signature. IPAB is automatically funded without annual appropriations from Congress, and its actions are not subject to administrative or judicial review.[25] All of this is so obviously unconstitutional that one wonders whether anyone in Congress or the Obama administration really believed it would ever function as advertised.

Meanwhile, the Obama administration and the Democrats turned out to have grossly misjudged matters in thinking they would retain full control of Congress, and that Obamacare would become increasingly popular. Obama managed to win reelection in 2012, but Republicans took control of the House of Representatives in 2010 and the Senate in 2014. This meant that Obama would need Republican cooperation to fix any errors in Obamacare, or to modify any provisions that turned out to be especially unpopular.

Instead of proposing compromise with the Republicans, the Obama administration has, in direct violation of the Constitution's requirement that the president take care to see that the laws are faithfully executed, simply decided to unilaterally delay, modify, and ignore various provisions of the law. Many of these actions were undertaken for transparently political reasons.[26] For example, Obamacare requires most employers with more than fifty employees to provide an approved insurance plan to their workers by January 1, 2014, or pay a fine per uninsured employee. By 2013, it became apparent that many smaller companies were planning to abandon whatever insurance coverage they had previously provided employees, pay the relatively small fine, and dump their employees onto the Obamacare exchanges, where many of them would qualify for federal subsidies.

To avoid this impending political disaster, on July 2, 2013, the Obama administration announced, in a Treasury Department blog post, that for employers with between fifty and ninety-nine employees the insurance mandate would be postponed until

2015—not coincidentally, after the 2014 midterm elections.[27] Meanwhile, the administration, with absolutely no legal authority to do so, issued rules requiring any employer who took advantage of the delay to not subsequently reduce or eliminate health insurance and throw its employees onto the exchanges. In March 2014, the administration delayed full implementation of the employer mandate until 2016.[28]

Similarly, the president's "if you like your plan you can keep it" lie became a massive political headache for the Democrats in the fall of 2013. Many individuals and businesses who had insured themselves outside of group plans received cancellation notices from their insurance company because their plans did not meet "minimum essential coverage" requirements under Obamacare. On November 14, 2013, the Obama administration issued guidance encouraging state insurance commissioners to allow existing non-Obamacare-compliant plans that were in effect on October 1, 2013, to continue through October 1, 2014.[29] Remarkably, the Obama administration was asking insurance commissioners to disobey federal law. In December, President Obama announced that the federal government would not enforce the individual mandate in 2014 against people whose insurance policies were canceled due to Obamacare.[30] On March 5, 2014, the administration asked state insurance commissioners not to enforce Obamacare rules that would require existing plans to fold until October 1, 2016—again, not surprisingly, well after the 2014 midterm elections. Nothing in the statute gave the president the authority to waive the relevant mandatory deadlines.

South Texas College of Law professor Josh Blackman aptly calls the administration's unilateral announcements of changes to Obamacare "government by blog post," a completely unconstitutional way of governing.[31] Obama preferred governing this way even when Republicans offered to work with him. Before Obama announced that he would ignore the law and allow the grandfathering of otherwise unlawful health care plans, Republicans proposed a bill that would have grandfathered existing plans. The president announced he would veto any such bill.[32]

The Obama administration claimed that its Obamacare delays were consistent with the president's traditional discretion to decide when and how to enforce the law. University of Michigan law professor Nicholas Bagley, who generally supports Obamacare, eviscerated this argument.[33] Bagley acknowledged that presidents have some authority to delay implementing statutes when they are short of enforcement resources. But the Obamacare delays instead reflected "the administration's policy-based anxiety over the pace at which the ACA was supposed to go into effect." The administration encouraged "a large portion of the regulated population to violate a statute in the service of broader policy goals."[34]

The administration also claims that with regard to the employer mandate delays, it was simply following an established IRS practice of giving "transitional relief" to taxpayers who are having difficulty complying immediately with changes to the tax code. As Bagley points out, however, such transitional relief typically affects only a few taxpayers, and exists for only a few months at most. It therefore provides only very limited support for "a sweeping exemption that will relieve thousands of employers from a substantial" tax burden for two years. Bagley concluded that the Obama administration has adopted a theory that would "mark a major shift of constitutional power away from Congress, which makes the laws, and toward the President, who is supposed to enforce them."[35]

Similarly, law professor Zachary Price notes that the Obama administration willfully violated America's "deeply rooted constitutional tradition" that "presidents, unlike English kings, lack authority to suspend statutes."[36] Price adds that absent "a clear statutory basis, an executive waiver of statutory requirements" is "presumptively impermissible." Unfortunately, it's generally very difficult to find a plaintiff with legal standing to challenge the president's actions.

A different courtroom controversy, however, also involving the abuse of executive power, almost undermined Obamacare. When Obamacare was being drafted, its authors expected that every state would set up an insurance exchange that would allow individual purchasers to buy insurance from among a variety of options. As it turned out, however, public opposition to Obamacare meant that most states refused to set up their own exchanges.

Obamacare provided that if states failed to set up their own exchanges, the federal government must set up exchanges for them. The law, however, only provides for subsidies for low-income individuals who buy insurance on exchanges "established by a state." Nevertheless, the Internal Revenue Service implemented regulations decreeing that individuals would be eligible for subsidies regardless of whether their insurance came from a state or federal exchange. The IRS failed to cite any meaningful legal authority for that conclusion.

Once the rule became the subject of political controversy, Obamacare's defenders argued that the language limiting subsidies to exchanges established by individual states was a mere "scrivener's error." "Established by a state" should be interpreted to mean "established by a state or by the federal government," because that is the only logical way to interpret the statute. In response, Case Western University law professor Jonathan Adler and the Cato Institute's Michael Cannon, who had been among the first to notice the rogue language, argued that Congress meant to bribe potentially recalcitrant states to establish exchanges; whether a state established an exchange or not, its citizens could still buy health insurance on an exchange, but only citizens of states that created their own exchanges would get subsidies.

Adler and Cannon pointed out that this sort of coercive bribery was very similar to how Obamacare handled Medicaid expansion.

Their critics swore up and down that no one had such bribery in mind, and that everyone understood that exchanges "established by a state" would include "state exchanges created by the federal government." This claim has been undermined by several videos unearthed by Obamacare opponents featuring MIT professor Jonathan Gruber, one of the main architects of Obamacare. In those videos, Gruber explained that Obamacare threatened states that if they failed to establish exchanges, their citizens would be deprived of subsidies.[37]

Meanwhile, no evidence appeared supporting the IRS's interpretation of the law. The IRS failed to respond to a House Oversight Committee subpoena requesting documents that would shed light on its claim that it used legislative history in determining the meaning of "established by a state."[38] Congressional Democrats did not produce a single internal document, email, briefing paper, or anything else that supports the proposition that everyone—or anyone—understood exchanges "established by a state" to include exchanges established by the federal government. At best, it seems that in the rush to get Obamacare through the Senate in December 2009, no one noticed that the law failed to provide for low-income subsidies if states failed to create exchanges. At worst (for the administration), Adler and Cannon are right, and Obamacare's drafters intended for subsidies to be available only to citizens of states that created exchanges.

If the litigation that attended this controversy involved ordinary legislation, there seems to be little question that the courts would have given the statute its natural reading—subsidies are not available to federally created exchanges, and it's up to Congress to amend the law to provide such subsidies, if it so desires.[39] And indeed, when the Supreme Court decided the case in June 2015, all nine justices agreed that "the most natural reading of the pertinent statutory phrase" is that subsidies are available only in states that have set up their own exchanges.[40]

Nevertheless, Chief Justice John Roberts, writing for a 6–3 majority, concluded that "the context and structure of the act" dictated that the Court depart from the plain meaning of the statutory language. Essentially, Roberts argued that allowing the language of the law to undermine Obamacare would be a "calamitous result" that Congress could not have intended.

That much is self-evidently true; no one drafts a law hoping that one part of the law will wind up undermining the rest of it. Roberts then made a questionable leap in logic, that it is therefore the Court's duty to read the relevant "established by a state" language in a way that preserves Obamacare's functionality, to allow exchanges established by the federal government to sell policies eligible for subsidies. Roberts in effect substituted a legislative role (changing the meaning of a statute for practical reasons) for a judicial one (interpreting a statute). In dissent, Justice Antonin Scalia expressed his frustration at the Court's linguistic manipulations. "Words no longer have meaning," he wrote, "if an Exchange that is not established by a State is 'established by the State.'"[41]

This chapter has described only some of the most egregious examples of the Obama administration's violations of the rule of law and the Constitution in passing and implementing Obamacare. Much more could be written about the illegal bullying and shaking down of health insurance companies;[42] accounting tricks used to evade budget rules that would have strangled Obamacare in its crib;[43] Obamacare waivers for seemingly arbitrary reasons to various groups;[44] bogus rulemaking that allowed members of Congress and their staffs to evade Obamacare requirements;[45] funding shenanigans by the Department of Health and Human Services;[46] additional changes, delays, and modifications to Obamacare outside the normal legislative and administrative process;[47] and more.

Chapter 7

YOU CAN'T SAY THAT!

IMAGINE THAT THE SUPREME COURT issues an opinion holding that the First Amendment protects the right to show a movie criticizing a presidential candidate before an election. The president and other leading members of his party respond by lying about the opinion's scope; vilifying individuals and groups on the other side of the political spectrum poised to exercise the rights recognized by the Supreme Court; siccing the IRS on those groups; and proposing to amend the Constitution to upend the Supreme Court's decision even if it means severely undermining the First Amendment. You don't have to imagine any of this, because it's exactly what happened with the Supreme Court's 2010 decision in the *Citizens United* case.[1]

Starting in the 1970s, the Supreme Court, while allowing some restrictions on donations to political campaigns, held that private individuals and corporations are entitled to a fair degree of protection under the First Amendment when they seek to spend money to advocate for one side or another of a political campaign. After all, depriving people of the means to express their views would be a very effective way of shutting them up.

Over time, support for government regulation of campaign donations and spending has become a significant "cause" on the liberal left. Some of this opposition arises from a sense that money plays too large a role in American politics, is corrupting, and puts a thumb on the political scale in favor of the well-to-do. It's not at all clear that there really is "too much money" in politics—as columnist George Will likes to point out, Americans spend approximately the same amount of money on politicking during an election year as they do annually on potato chips —but many Americans sincerely believe there is.

Politicians, however, aren't known for their sincerity. And Democratic politicians from the president on down, along with allied activist groups, have a more pressing, practical reason to want the government to clamp down on campaign spending— they want to dry up an important source of opposition to their policies.[2] Liberals dominate most of the leading opinion-making areas of American life—journalism, the movie and television industries, academia, the publishing industry, the legal profession, the mainline churches, and the arts. Conservatives dominate talk radio, evangelical churches, and have Fox News, but that hardly evens things out.

By contrast with liberal dominance in the opinion-making elite, the playing field is more or less level with regard to spending on political campaigns—on average, Democrats and Republicans spend approximately the same amount. Neither party has the massive, structural advantages when it comes to campaign spending that the Democrats have in the broader political and ideological arena. Without the relatively level playing field of campaign spending, left-leaning opinion-makers would be able to virtually monopolize American political discourse.

So the Obama administration's and leading Democratic politicians' over-the-top reaction to *Citizens United* was not because they suddenly became Boy Scouts interested in improving the American political system by reducing the relevance of money— indeed, in 2008 Obama, breaking a campaign promise, became the first major-party candidate to decline federal campaign funds and the spending limits that come with those funds. His campaign wound up outspending McCain's by the largest margin in history.³ Rather, the Democrats understand that reducing the funds available to all candidates will disproportionately harm the Republicans, because Republicans have fewer "free" ways to get their message out.

In January 2010, the Supreme Court decided *Citizens United*. The Court held that a part of the McCain-Feingold campaign finance law that restricted "independent expenditures" on political campaigns by corporations and labor unions violated the First Amendment. Citizens United, an incorporated conservative political group, had wanted to pay television stations to advertise a film it produced that was critical of Hillary Clinton. This violated Section 203 of McCain-Feingold, which prohibited corporations and unions from spending money on broadcast "electioneering communications" that mention a candidate's name, if those communications would occur within thirty days of a primary or sixty days of a general election involving that candidate. This ban applied even if the communication was not meant to influence the outcome of the election. The government acknowledged that the law even prohibited Walmart from advertising candidate dolls less than sixty days before an election.

To anyone who believes in freedom of speech, such overbearing restrictions should be troubling. But the Obama administration made the government's pro-restriction argument even more dubious. McCain-Feingold's electioneering communications ban applied only to broadcasts. When *Citizens United* was argued before the Supreme Court, Chief Justice Roberts asked the government's attorney whether, consistent with the Constitution, the law could be amended to also ban books and pamphlets. The government's lawyer said yes. "That's pretty incredible," Justice Alito responded. "You think that if a book was published, a campaign biography that was the functional equivalent of express advocacy, that could be banned?"[4] Yes, replied the government's advocate, and that wasn't all.

Roberts then more specifically asked if the government could prohibit a corporation from publishing a five-hundred-page political book that concluded with a single line saying "vote for X." The government's lawyer answered that if the book was funded directly by the corporation, and not through a political action committee, "we could prohibit publication of the book." Justice Scalia, stupefied by the breadth of the government's claimed power of censorship, lashed out at the government's attorney: "I'm a little disoriented here, Mr. Stewart. We are dealing with a constitutional provision, are we not; the one that I remember which says Congress shall make no law abridging the freedom of the press? That's what we're interpreting here?" The only reply he received was "that's correct."[5]

The Court took the unusual step of ordering reargument. Solicitor General (and future Supreme Court Justice) Elena Kagan, now arguing for the government, stated that the government had narrowed its position. Kagan pointed out that the Federal Elections Commission had never tried to restrict the publication of books.[6] Kagan added that the law would be subject to "quite good" challenges if it were ever applied to books. Chief Justice Roberts immediately seized on this, saying, "We don't put our First Amendment rights in the hands of FEC bureaucrats." Kagan then acknowledged that the government believed that it could ban corporate and union spending on pamphlets, because "a pamphlet is pretty classic electioneering." She also admitted that the government thought that it could ban a book advocating for a candidate if it resembled a lengthy pamphlet.[7]

The Supreme Court ruled against the government 5–4, along standard liberal-conservative ideological lines, with the conservatives championing free speech and the liberals opposing it.

Citizens United did not disturb rules regulating corporate contributions directly to candidates' campaigns. Rather, it held that Congress may not ban Americans from contributing money to nonprofit advocacy corporations, which in turn use the money to promote their donors' concerns.

President Obama immediately lambasted the decision. The White House issued a press release accusing the Supreme Court of giving "a green light to a new stampede of special interest money in our politics. It is a major victory for big oil, Wall Street banks, health insurance companies and the other powerful interests that marshal their power every day in Washington."[8]

Liberal politicians and activist groups misrepresented the opinion as holding for the first time that corporations have the same constitutional rights as people. The Supreme Court did so in *Citizens United*, they alleged, to help corporate fat cats take over American politics at the expense of the progressive agenda. In fact, Supreme Court precedent going back well over a century held that corporations could assert rights, including First Amendment rights, under the Constitution, and *Citizens United* made no mention of corporate personhood.[9] The majority instead focused on the content of the speech, not on the speaker, and held instead that political speech does not lose First Amendment protection "simply because its source is a corporation." Otherwise, there would be nothing in the Constitution stopping the government from shutting down any newspaper, movie company, television station, or website that organized itself as a corporation.

Speaking of newspapers and websites, few if any of *Citizens United*'s most vigorous opponents suggest that large, extremely influential liberal media conglomerates like the *New York Times* or the *Huffington Post* should face government restrictions regarding when and to what extent they may engage in political advocacy. Yet such corporations are more influential than all of the nonmedia corporate advocacy groups put together.

President Obama embraced and encouraged demagoguery over *Citizens United*. A week after the decision came out, the president delivered his State of the Union address with most of the Supreme Court justices present. Obama once again attacked the Court over *Citizens United*. "With all due deference to separation of powers, last week the Supreme Court reversed a century of law that, I believe, will open the floodgates for special interests, including foreign corporations, to spend without limit in our elections," Obama said. Justice Samuel Alito, agitated that the president inaccurately suggested that the case allowed foreign corporations to spend money on American elections, mouthed "not true."[10] We know that the president was not interested in the truth, however, because he continued to repeat this falsehood well beyond the point that any reasonable person could believe it.[11]

While the president's speech provided red meat to partisan Democrats, many observers were troubled by the president's lack of decorum not just in taking such a harsh swipe at the Supreme Court—something that no president had done with such vigor for over seventy years—but in doing so with the justices sitting in front of him. The justices were barred by protocol from objecting in any way, and had to sit there quietly like children while the president scolded them. That's no way, many critics argued, to treat a coequal branch of government.[12]

Worse was yet to come. While denouncing *Citizens United* in August 2010, President Obama libeled Americans for Prosperity, a pro–free market organization founded by the billionaire libertarian Koch (pronounced "Coke") brothers, Charles and David, owners of Koch Industries, the second-largest privately held company in the United States. Obama said, "Right now all around this country there are groups with harmless-sounding names like Americans for Prosperity, who are running millions of dollars of ads . . . And they don't have to say who exactly the Americans for

Prosperity are. You don't know if it's a foreign-controlled corporation."[13] As President Obama well knew, Americans for Prosperity is not a foreign-controlled corporation.

In September, Obama senior advisor David Axelrod declared outright, and in an outright lie, that the "benign-sounding Americans for Prosperity, the American Crossroads fund" are "front groups for foreign-controlled companies."[14] That tactic never got any traction. Even liberal-leaning news organizations pointed out both that *Citizens United* did not involve foreign corporations, and that it was absurd to allege that American conservative groups were fronts for such corporations.

The Democratic establishment decided that if they were unable to stifle conservative donors through campaign finance legislation, they would do it through other means. Leading Democrats, including the president himself, embarked on an extraordinary, wide-ranging campaign to demonize the Koch brothers. The brothers had long been involved in promoting libertarian ideology and, more recently, in Republican politics. When the attacks on them started, the Kochs had been spending around ten to fifteen million dollars per year to promote libertarian ideology and to help Republican candidates.[15] The Kochs' most effective journalistic critic alleged that over a period of many years, the Kochs had given a total of "over one hundred million dollars" to "right-wing causes."[16]

The notion that these contributions were distorting American politics is ridiculous. The 2008 Obama campaign spent over seven hundred million dollars, while the 2010 federal midterm elections cost about four billion dollars. The Koch's ten- to fifteen-million-dollar annual contribution to that spending was like spitting in an ocean. With regard to the Kochs' more general influence on the nation's ideological climate, liberals hold the vast majority of academic positions in almost every humanities and social science department in every major university in the country, with total budgets in the tens of billions of dollars. Even in the libertarians' tiny corner of the ideological universe, ten million dollars would only keep the Cato Institute, the leading libertarian think tank cofounded by Charles Koch, running for three months a year, and leave nothing for any other libertarian cause or organization.

Nevertheless, Democrats decided to latch on to the Kochs as their bogeymen. They figured mysterious (because generally adverse to publicity), ominous-sounding (billionaires! involved in the oil industry!) villains on whom to blame their troubles and rouse the passions of their partisans would be useful. Ironically, the Kochs, rightly feeling they had been unfairly attacked, increased their political spending dramatically.

The war on the Kochs started with a hit piece in the *New Yorker* in August 2010 by Jane Mayer.[17] This was not a purely spontaneous journalistic endeavor by Mayer, but one in part plotted and supported by the very sort of big money politicos Mayer was supposedly exposing. A substantial amount of her research was provided by Lee Fang of ThinkProgress, a Beltway institution with very close ties to the Obama White House and the Democratic establishment.[18] While accusing the Kochs of hiding their activism by "creating slippery organizations with generic-sounding names," Mayer favorably cited slippery *left-wing* organizations with generic-sounding names that were out to get the Kochs for political reasons, including the Center for Public Integrity, Media Matters, and the National Committee for Responsive Philanthropy.

Nor did Mayer provide some relevant context: compared to the $100 million or so the Kochs had spent on politics over many years, liberal billionaire George Soros spends about $150 million a year to "support individuals and organizations advancing a more open, just, and equal society in the United States."[19] Meanwhile, the liberal Ford Foundation spends over $400 million annually, and the liberal MacArthur Foundation spends about $140 million a year.

A few weeks after Mayer's article appeared, Austan Goolsbee, the president's economic advisor, told conference-call participants that "in this country we have partnerships, we have S corps, we have LLCs, we have a series of entities that do not pay corporate income tax. Some of which are really giant firms, you know Koch Industries is a multibillion dollar businesses . . ."[20] Goolsbee said that he thought that Koch Industries was a "pass-through entity," information that he could only have received from the Internal Revenue Service.[21]

IRS disclosure of such information is illegal. The Obama administration, after first falsely suggesting that Goolsbee was relying on publicly available information, later claimed that he had misspoken, and had merely used the Kochs as an inaccurate example of a broader problem. Several years later, Goolsbee claimed that he mistakenly relied on a seven-year-old article about the Kochs' third brother, who has no stake in Koch Industries.[22] Making matters worse, according to Koch Industries' attorney the company does in fact pay income taxes, so whatever information Goolsbee thought he was relying on was false or incomplete. Under congressional pressure, the administration ultimately agreed to conduct an internal investigation into Goolsbee's comment, but it refused to release the results.[23]

The Goolsbee incident taught the Obama administration that it was too risky for it to go after the Kochs directly and have the administration involved in false or exaggerated mudslinging against private citizens. Other parts of the Democratic machine instead took the lead. In September 2010, the Democratic Congressional Campaign Committee claimed on its website that the Kochs have "funneled their money into right-wing shadow groups."[24] A week later, Representative Chris Van Hollen, chairman of the Democratic Congressional Campaign Committee, falsely accused Koch Industries of "outsourcing" and claimed that "they actually got an award for 'outsourcing' to China."[25]

Meanwhile, the Obama administration was quietly encouraging a media blitz against the Kochs. The *Huffington Post* reported that a senior administration official, speaking to a gathering of reporters, urged them to attack the Kochs. "The Koch brothers may be Republican ideologues," he said, "but they are oilmen too. You read Jane Mayer's piece, they are talking about feeding the Tea Party rallies. They are [pushing] information about the insidious nature of the EPA [Environmental Protection Agency]. This isn't just a philosophical deal. This is special interests using the process in a way that they have never been able to use before, to try and push their agenda, to try and reverse the gains we have made here on behalf of everyday people and the country as a whole."[26]

In George Orwell's dystopian novel *1984*, the ruling party told the public that their primary enemy was a shadowy figure named Emmanuel Goldstein. Goldstein, responsible for all the ills of society, was the subject of a daily "two minutes hate." The Kochs have become the Emmanuel Goldsteins of the Obama administration. Since Mayer's piece came out, they've been blamed for everything from global warming[27] to public school segregation[28] to the proposed Keystone pipeline[29] to Trayvon Martin's death at the hands of George Zimmerman[30] to voter ID laws[31] to the battles between the state government and municipal unions in Wisconsin. The underlying accusations were at best exaggerated, and more often were completely false.

The Obama administration was sometimes directly complicit in the attacks on the Kochs. For example, in early 2011 the White House sent Obama for America political operatives to Wisconsin to try to insert the Kochs into media coverage of state political battles. The president's reelection campaign several times mailed fundraising letters attacking the Kochs, in one case depicting them as "plotting oil men" who are bent on "misleading people" with "disinformation" to "smear the President's record."[32] On April 13, 2011, Lee Fang published an article at ThinkProgress falsely accusing the Kochs of illegally manipulating oil and gas prices.[33] By remarkable coincidence (not!), the Obama administration was forming a task force on fraud and manipulation in the gas market at exactly the same time; the task force was formally announced on April 21.[34] Less directly, President Obama, as the head of the Democratic Party, could have ordered the party apparatus to call off its attack dogs. Instead, throughout the 2012 election campaign various Democratic fundraising committees used the Kochs as fundraising bait.

The most egregious and persistent attacks on the Koch brothers came from then–Senate Majority Leader Harry Reid, a Nevada Democrat. Beginning in early 2014, he launched almost daily (and often factually inaccurate) verbal assaults on the Kochs, and also established a website dedicated to the Kochs' purported misdeeds. To get an idea of the tenor of the site, a page headlined "meet the Kochs" introduces them as "producers of toxic chemicals, harmful pollutants, carcinogens, greenhouse gases."[35] Among other insults, Reid called the brothers "un-American"[36] and "power-hungry tycoons."[37] He mentioned them in Senate speeches well over one hundred times.[38] When Texas Republican Ted Cruz accused Reid of launching "an unprecedented slander campaign against two private citizens," Reid spokesman Alan Jentleson retorted that Cruz was "rushing to the defense of shadowy billionaires who are rigging our democracy to benefit the wealthy and powerful."[39]

The wide-ranging effort to demonize two private citizens for exercising their First Amendment rights in ways contrary to the interests of one political party should be of concern to all Americans. The Kochs have faced persistent death threats as a result of the hate campaign conducted against them.[40] Speaking up, even as loudly as the Kochs do, should not result in the government figuratively putting a price on the speakers' head, supported by false and exaggerated allegations against them.

But intimidation was the whole point of the exercise. As the *Wall Street Journal*'s Kim Strassel explains, the Democrats attacked the Kochs to warn other potential Republican donors that they would face a public smearing if they donated to GOP campaigns.[41] Indeed, at the same time that the Democrats were plotting their war against the Kochs, congressional Democrats, with the cooperation of the White House, were pushing a new law called the "DISCLOSE Act" that would make it easier for them to identify, and then bully, other Republican donors. The act's sponsor, Senator Charles Schumer, acknowledged that the idea behind the proposed law was to make corporate donors "think twice" and to have a "deterrent effect."[42]

The American Civil Liberties Union condemned the bill, arguing that it "would inflict unnecessary damage to free speech rights and does not include the proper safeguards to protect Americans' privacy. The bill would severely impact donor anonymity, especially those donors who give to smaller and more controversial organizations."[43] The House of Representatives passed the DISCLOSE Act, but it died in the Senate.

The Democratic establishment's other gambit to unlevel the political playing field was to encourage an IRS crackdown on so-called 501(c)(4) corporations. Section 501(c)(4) of the Internal Revenue Code allows organizations "operated primarily for the purpose of bringing about civic betterments and social improvements" to organize as nontaxable entities. Unlike 501(c)(3) charities, contributions to 501(c)(4)s are not tax deductible. The IRS allows 501(c)(4)s to engage in political activity so long as more than 50 percent of their resources are devoted to other things.

After *Citizens United*, Democrats became concerned that major Republican donors would use 501(c)(4)s to funnel money to Republican candidates, offsetting Democratic support from labor unions, which typically are organized as 501(c)(5)s. Meanwhile, many new conservative Tea Party groups were springing up, creating a grassroots danger for Democrats facing election battles in 2010 and 2012.

The IRS faced pressure from Senate Democrats such as Michael Bennet, Dick Durbin, Carl Levin, Al Franken, Jeff Merkley, Chuck Schumer, Jeanne Shaheen, Tom Udall, and Sheldon Whitehouse,[44] various House Democrats,[45] and several liberal pressure groups,[46] to crack down on conservative 501(c)(4)s. IRS Director of Exempt Organizations Lois Lerner emailed a subordinate, "The Supreme Court dealt a huge blow, overturning a 100-year old precedent that basically corporations couldn't give directly to political campaigns. And everyone is up in arms because they don't like it. The Federal Election Commission can't do anything about it. They want the IRS to fix the problem."[47]

That pressure, combined with the liberal leanings of its own staff, including Lerner, led the IRS to scrutinize 501(c)(4) applications from groups that seemed to be conservative (groups with "Tea Party" in their name, for example, but also groups that engaged in "anti-Obama rhetoric"),[48] much more closely than they scrutinized applications from groups with liberal- or neutral-sounding names.[49] The IRS asked applicants for 501(c)(4) status for voluminous and often inappropriate information, and for a time it was virtually impossible for conservative groups to win the agency's approval to establish themselves as 501(c)(4)s.

As the Center for Competitive Politics reports, "In many cases, the IRS required that groups send the agency their donor lists, names of board members, copies of minutes from all board meetings, resumes of individuals involved in the organization, and copies of all social media postings. Some organizations were asked to provide reports about the books their members had read as a group. Others were asked about their relationship to other groups and to politically engaged individuals. In some cases, organizations were asked about what kinds of activities they would participate in [in] the future. Organizations were even told to provide personal information on seasonal interns and to provide copies of all correspondence with former interns. Making matters worse, each of the questionnaires contained a letter threatening perjury charges for providing the wrong information, which is especially troubling when considering that, in some instances, the responses were over an astounding twenty thousand pages in length."[50] Many of those who tried to organize 501(c)(4)s eventually gave up, some out of frustration, others because they did not have the resources to comply with the never-ending paperwork requests. Meanwhile, leaders of some of the groups, along with conservative activists such as Delaware Republican senatorial candidate Christine O'Donnell—whose tax information, the IRS acknowledged, was "improperly accessed"—claimed that they were subjected to retaliatory audits by the IRS and investigations by other government agencies.[51]

Word of IRS harassment spread through conservative circles, was covered by conservative blogs and talk shows, and raised concerns among some Senate and House Republicans.[52] But the establishment media ignored the scandal. They did so in part because IRS officials repeatedly lied to Congress, testifying that there was no program targeting conservative 501(c)(4)s.

The establishment media also attributed claims of IRS harassment of Tea Party and other conservative groups to conservative paranoia about President Obama. But, as the saying goes, just because you're paranoid doesn't mean that no one is out to get you. The IRS publicly admitted that it had targeted conservative groups in May 2013.

That the IRS put its massive bureaucratic thumb on the scales against conservative activist groups is one of the great political scandals in recent American history. Lerner and many of her top aides managed to delete, destroy, or otherwise lose access to much of their correspondence related to the scandal, so it may be years before we know for sure whether anyone in the White House was directly involved, if ever.

We do know there was at least one highly unusual and seemingly inappropriate meeting between President Obama and IRS Chief Counsel William Wilkins in 2012, just two days before the latter's office released new guidelines for scrutinizing Tea Party groups.[53] At the very least, President Obama's persistent attacks on "shadowy" conservative groups for exercising rights the Supreme Court deemed protected by the First Amendment helped create the political atmosphere in which IRS abuses thrived.

President Obama expressed appropriate outrage when the IRS scandal came to light, telling the public that he "will not tolerate this kind of behavior in any agency but especially in the IRS, given the power that it has and the reach that it has into all of our lives."[54] He ordered Attorney General Eric Holder to conduct a criminal investigation into possible wrongdoing.

But Obama's initial bark was much louder than his bite, and for that matter was much louder than his later bark. Holder appointed Barbara Bosserman, a donor to Obama campaigns and the Democratic National Committee, to run the probe.[55] Many people took this as a signal that the administration was not terribly interested in getting to the bottom of the controversy.[56] Lawyers for conservative 501(c)(4) groups targeted by the IRS later announced that no one from the Justice Department had contacted them, raising questions regarding exactly how seriously the government was probing IRS misbehavior.

By the time Fox News's Bill O'Reilly interviewed the president in February 2014, nine months after the IRS admitted wrongdoing, Obama was downplaying the scandal. Obama told O'Reilly, falsely, that the scandal was the result of "bone-headed decisions . . . out of a local office." Obama was alluding to the IRS Cincinnati office, though he knew or should have known that Lois Lerner had ordered applications by Tea Party groups that arrived in Cincinnati to be sent to IRS headquarters in Washington, D.C.[57] Obama added that there "isn't a smidgen of evidence" of corruption in the scandal—a rather rash conclusion, given that the investigation was still ongoing.[58]

Moreover, Obama's Treasury Department, rather than taking the IRS scandal as evidence that the agency couldn't be trusted to regulate political matters, as the IRS's own National Taxpayer Advocate concluded,[59] instead proposed detailed new IRS rules for regulating the political activities of 501(c)(4)s. The proposed rules would dramatically increase the agency's role in regulating political speech. This proved too much even for many liberals, and the proposal met with strong opposition across the political spectrum. Nan Aron, president of the Alliance for Justice, a coalition of over one hundred progressive groups, alleged that the proposed rules would "quash democratic participation" by social welfare organizations.[60]

The Democrats' most recent effort to regulate campaign spending came in the form of a reckless proposed constitutional amendment that would have allowed Congress and the states to "regulate and set reasonable limits on the raising and spending of money by candidates and others to influence elections." This amendment, which passed the Senate 54–42 in September 2014, failing the needed two-thirds vote, would have gone well beyond overturning *Citizens United* and allowing regulation of corporate spending on politicking close to election time. Rather, any spending, by any corporation or individual, would be subject to "reasonable limits" if the goal of the spending was to "influence elections."

The amendment, then, was the most significant attack on freedom of speech in decades. The American Civil Liberties Union declared, without exaggeration, that, if passed, it would "fundamentally 'break' the Constitution and endanger civil rights and civil liberties for generations."[61] Yet every Democratic senator who cast a vote favored the amendment.

Few if any of these senators likely intended that government be empowered to engage in censorship so long as they could persuade the courts that it was "reasonable." But as Republican Senator Ted Cruz pointed out, "what we are debating is not the intentions of one hundred Senators. What we are debating is a constitutional amendment that . . . Democrats are proposing to be inserted into the Bill of Rights."[62] Cruz noted that, in the past, liberal stalwarts such as the late Senator Ted Kennedy vehemently opposed similar attempts to tinker with the First Amendment.

The ACLU is virtually the last holdout on the left supporting freedom of speech in political campaigns. Its progressive constituency, however, is pressuring it to abandon that position. The Obama administration's and the Democratic establishment's abandonment of freedom of speech to seek short-term political gain—not just in supporting the amendment, but in attacking the Koch brothers to intimidate Republican donors, and in at least tolerating and in some cases encouraging IRS harassment of conservative political organizations—bodes ill for the future.

Chapter 8

ANTIDISCRIMINATION LAW RUN AMOK

THE OBAMA ADMINISTRATION has pursued the enforcement of antidiscrimination laws in ways that invade Americans' rights to freedom of religion, freedom of speech, and due process of law. Consider first the administration's assault on religious freedom in a case called *Hosanna-Tabor Evangelical Lutheran Church v. EEOC*.

For most of American history, the right of religious communities to choose their leadership went unquestioned. In part, this was because employment in general was "at will"—an employer, including a religious employer, could hire or fire any employee for any reason or no reason. And in part, this was because Americans believed that protecting the autonomy of religious organizations was an important aspect of religious freedom. And few things strike closer to the heart of religious freedom than the right of churches and other religious organizations to decide who serves as clergy and otherwise teaches and represents the faith.

Slowly but surely, however, both factors have eroded. Federal, state, and local laws now protect employees from discrimination based on a wide range of criteria, including race, sex, pregnancy, age, disability, and, in some jurisdictions, anything from sexual orientation to political affiliation to membership in a motorcycle gang. Many people think the right to be free from private-sector discrimination is at least as important as preserving religious freedom from government encroachment. Meanwhile, more and more Americans see religious institutions, especially those that stick to traditionalist theology, as reactionary, patriarchal, and oppressive. As such, they not only don't deserve autonomy, but should be considered ripe for reform or even suppression via antidiscrimination and other laws.

Nevertheless, through the Obama administration, federal courts consistently held that the First Amendment protects the right of religious organizations to choose their religious staff free from the interference of secular law. The courts either concluded that this right was part of the amendment's guarantee of freedom of religion, or that to rule otherwise would unconstitutionally entangle the courts in religious matters in violation of the amendment's prohibition on government establishment of religion. Some courts ruled in favor of religious autonomy for both reasons.

The right to choose religious staff became known as the "ministerial exception," and the only real controversy in the courts was how broadly the exception should apply. It obviously applied to actual clergy—ministers, priests, imams, and rabbis— but what about church organists? Sunday school teachers? Administrative staff?

Several religious day schools found themselves in legal trouble when they fired teachers for violating church teachings. Some teachers sued even though they had agreed in writing that part of their job was to serve as role models for the children regarding church doctrine.

Courts divided on the issue of whether a religious school may lawfully fire a married pregnant teacher who wishes to keep teaching in contravention of the school's religiously based view that mothers with young children should not work outside the home. A federal appellate court held that the school had a constitutional right protected by the ministerial exception to fire such a teacher, while the Michigan Supreme Court concluded that, even if the ministerial exemption applied, it was overridden by the government's compelling interest in eradicating discrimination.[1]

Other cases involved religious schools firing unmarried teachers of secular subjects who became pregnant out of wedlock—such pregnancies being compelling evidence of a violation of the schools' religious teachings against premarital sex. Courts agreed that firing teachers under such circumstances violated laws banning sex and pregnancy discrimination, but courts disagreed on whether the schools were exempted from the antidiscrimination laws because of the ministerial exemption. Some courts said yes,[2] while others concluded that because the teachers in question primarily taught secular subjects, they did not qualify for the ministerial exception.[3]

To the extent that the ministerial exemption did not apply to teachers at religious schools, it left religious schools with two bad options: either employ teachers who violated church teachings and undermine the principle that part of their teachers' job is to serve as religious role models, or risk a lawsuit by enforcing school rules regarding adherence to church doctrine.

The Supreme Court finally agreed to hear a case on the scope of the ministerial exception in 2011. The case involved the Hosanna-Tabor evangelical school, a private elementary school affiliated with the Lutheran Church–Missouri Synod, and former Hosanna-Tabor teacher Cheryl Perich. Perich had taught secular and religious subjects at the school, and occasionally led chapel. She developed narcolepsy and began the 2004–05 academic year on disability leave. In January, Perich informed the school principal that she was ready to return to work. He told her that the school had already hired a teacher for the rest of the year. He also expressed skepticism about her ability to return to work. The school eventually offered to pay part of her health insurance premiums if she would resign. After Perich refused the offer and threatened a lawsuit, the school fired her.

The federal government took up her cause during the waning years of the Bush administration. The Equal Employment Opportunity Commission filed a lawsuit alleging that the school violated the Americans with Disabilities Act by retaliating against her for pursuing an antidiscrimination claim. Hosanna-Tabor responded that the termination was protected by the ministerial exception because of Perich's religious duties at the school and her status within the church as a teacher "called" to God's service. She was, moreover, fired for a religious reason: violating a church tenet that disputes among church members should be resolved within the church.

The EEOC argued that Perich's discrimination claim was not subject to the ministerial exception. The trial court disagreed and held in favor of the school, but the Sixth Circuit Court of Appeals ruled in favor of Perich. The Court of Appeals held that because Perich's duties mostly were the same as those of lay teachers, the ministerial exception did not apply to her job. So *Hosanna-Tabor* presented the Supreme Court with a perfect opportunity to clarify the scope of the exception.

Before the Court could do so, it first had to contend with an unexpected argument from the government. The issue, the Obama Justice Department decided to argue, was not just that Perich's job did not qualify for the ministerial exception, but that the ministerial exception should be rejected entirely. So, for example, a very liberal jurisdiction such as San Francisco could require the Catholic Church to hire male nuns or female priests, and the church would have no constitutionally valid freedom of religion defense.

To say that the government's position was outside the mainstream would be a gross understatement. Though opposition to the ministerial exception has some purchase in the left-wing corridors of the legal academy,[4] from the time the exception first explicitly surfaced in 1972, every federal court that had considered whether to adopt the exception had done so.

The government tried to cushion the radical implications of its argument by contending that churches would not lose all protection against government intervention in employing clergy. Churches could still invoke a different First Amendment right, the right to join with others for expressive purposes, known as the right of expressive association. This was a rather weak and ironic argument, given that the leading Supreme Court case protecting expressive association, *Boy Scouts of America v. Dale*, was vigorously condemned by most liberal interest groups, lawyers, and academics, including lawyers who took high-level positions in the Obama administration. The odds that the Obama administration would have fought for a significant right to expressive association for churches if push came to shove are close to nil.

In any event, the justices were incredulous at the government's position that religious organizations get no more constitutional protection than any other employer that promotes a point of view. Chief Justice John Roberts asked the government's attorney, "Is the issue we are talking about here in the view of the United States any different than any other group of people who get together for an expressive right?" The attorney answered, "We think the basic contours of the inquiry are not different." "That's extraordinary," Justice Antonin Scalia chimed in. "We are talking here about the free exercise clause and about the establishment clause, and you say they have no special application?" Even Justice Elena Kagan, a liberal Obama appointee, piled on. "I, too, find that amazing," she said.[5]

Not surprisingly, the Court ruled 9–0 against the administration, endorsing the ministerial exception and holding that it protected Hosanna-Tabor from Perich's lawsuit.[6] The Court stressed that it was ruling only on an employment discrimination claim, and was not addressing any other type of lawsuit by a church employee, including such possible claims as breach of contract or "tortious conduct" against an employee by a religious employer. Such issues can be judged when they arise, the Court concluded.

Justice Samuel Alito, joined by Justice Kagan, wrote a separate opinion. Alito explained that the freedom to choose one's spiritual leaders was broader than merely the choice of "ministers," since some faiths do not follow that approach to religious governance. What courts must focus upon in such cases, Alito wrote, is "the function performed by persons who work for religious bodies," not their titles.

In another example of incredible overreach by the government, this one not yet addressed by the courts, in April 2011 the US Department of Education's Office of Civil Rights (OCR) sent a "Dear Colleague" letter to university officials that has essentially forced almost every university in the country to rewrite its student disciplinary code. The OCR required colleges to lower the level of proof needed to find students accused of sexual misconduct guilty. The letter also implicitly barred schools from providing accused students with a fair disciplinary process.[7]

The OCR was responding to a campaign by activists seeking to reduce the incidence of sexual assault on campus. That's a very worthy goal, but it raises the question of why sexual assault, a serious felony, is an issue for university authorities rather than for the police. The answer lies in Title IX of the 1972 Education Amendments to the 1964 Civil Rights Act, which prohibits sex discrimination at universities that receive federal funding, which means almost all universities.

Title IX is famous for forcing universities to upgrade their women's sports programs, but it goes well beyond that. Courts have held that sexual harassment is a form of sex discrimination, including when one student harasses another. Schools subject to Title IX are responsible for monitoring and preventing harassment. OCR concluded that, if Title IX requires universities to combat sexual harassment because it interferes with women's educational opportunities, universities must also battle sex-related violence, for the same reason.

The notion that combatting sexual assault on campus required drastic action by the federal government to force universities to change their policies relied on two premises: first, that there was an epidemic of sexual assault against women on college campuses, and, second, that universities often mishandled complaints about such assaults, with the perpetrators often subject to little if any punishment. The first premise is false. Sexual assault on campus, as elsewhere in society, is a serious problem, but sex crimes at universities, as elsewhere in society, have declined dramatically over the last twenty years. Figures bandied about by the Obama administration to the effect that one in five college women will be sexually assaulted massively exaggerate the problem's scope.[8] Moreover, in colleges as elsewhere, the vast majority of rapes are committed by a small group of sociopaths, not, as activists sometimes allege, by normal men emboldened by what the activists claim is a "rape culture" that permeates universities.[9] And finally, college women are actually less likely to be victimized by sexual assault than noncollege women of the same age.[10]

It's true, on the other hand, that campus disciplinary proceedings have often mishandled complaints of sexual assaults, usually erring on the side of the alleged perpetrator. In some cases, university officials have conspired to get an accused person off the hook, perhaps because he was a star athlete, or the child of a well-connected alumnus, or because the university wanted to avoid bad publicity by denying that an assault took place. More often, though, the problem is that the campus disciplinary rules were established to deal with relatively minor campus offenses such as cheating on exams, underage drinking, and the like, and the system is not competent to address serious violent crime.

A college student who wants to file a complaint of sexual assault within the campus disciplinary system informs a university employee such as an assistant dean for student life, or perhaps the Title IX coordinator. That person eventually forwards the complaint to a university disciplinary panel that may be composed of, for example, an associate dean with a master's degree in English literature, a professor of chemistry, and a senior majoring in anthropology. Unlike criminal prosecutors, members of the disciplinary panels do not have access to subpoena powers or to crime labs. They often have no experience in fact-finding, arbitration, conflict resolution, or any other relevant skill set. There is, to put it mildly, little reason to expect such panels to have the experience, expertise, and resources necessary to adjudicate a contested claim of sexual assault.

Making matters worse, most campus tribunals ban attorneys for the parties (even in an advisory capacity), rules of procedure and evidence are typically ad hoc, and no one can consult precedents because records of previous disputes are sealed due to privacy considerations. Campus "courts" therefore have an inherently kangarooish nature. Even trained police officers and prosecutors too often mishandle sexual assault cases, so it's not surprising that the amateurs running the show at universities tend to have a poor record. And indeed, some victims' advocacy groups, such as the Rape, Abuse and Incest National Network (RAINN), oppose having the government further encourage the campus judicial system to primarily handle campus sexual assault claims, because that means not treating rape as a serious crime.[11]

A logical solution, if federal intervention is indeed necessary, would be for OCR to mandate that universities encourage students who complain of sexual assault to report the assault immediately to the police, and that universities develop procedures to cooperate with police investigations. Concerns about victims' well-being when prosecutors decline to pursue a case could also be adjudicated in a real court, as a student could seek a civil protective order against her alleged assailant. OCR could have mandated or encouraged universities to cooperate with those civil proceedings, which in some cases might warrant excluding an alleged assailant from campus.

Instead, OCR doubled down on campus kangaroo courts, making them even more marsupial. First, OCR required universities to lower the standard of proof in disciplinary hearings from "clear and convincing" evidence to a lower "preponderance" of evidence.[12] Second, though cross-examination is among the core tools by which litigants reveal the truth, OCR "strongly discourages" schools from allowing the accused student to cross-examine his accuser, lest the accuser be traumatized by the questioning.

OCR guidance also discourages allowing an accused student's representative to cross-examine the accuser. Rather, a school "may choose, instead, to allow the parties to submit questions to a trained third party (e.g., the hearing panel) to ask the questions on their behalf." Even then, "OCR recommends that the third party screen the questions submitted by the parties and only ask those it deems appropriate and relevant to the case."[13]

OCR also forbade university disciplinary panels from considering an accusing student's sexual history with anyone other than the accused.[14] Over the last few decades, almost all American courts have limited the extent to which accused rapists can bring in the sexual past of an alleged victim. This ensures that rape trials are not in effect also putting the victim on trial. But no jurisdiction has adopted a blanket rule excluding *all* sexual history evidence not involving the accused. Such evidence is occasionally highly relevant, and a blanket rule would deprive the defendant in such cases of a valid defense.

Imagine, for example, that a video circulates around a college campus showing a man and a woman engaging in what most people would consider a degrading sex act for the woman. The woman then files a complaint with the university, claiming she was sexually assaulted. During the investigation, the woman claims she would never voluntarily consent to such a degrading act. The accused, however, locates four men willing to testify that they engaged in the exact same act with the accuser, and it was fully consensual. One of them even has his own video of the interaction. Under the OCR guidelines, the student accused of sexual assault would not be allowed to present that evidence.

OCR also states that a "school should also ensure that hearings are conducted in a manner that does not inflict additional trauma on the complainant," which implies that the school should not start the proceedings with a presumption of innocence, or even a stance of neutrality.[15] Rather, university officials should assume that any complaint is valid and the accused is guilty as charged.

Beyond issuing (unlawful) prospective guidelines for adjudicating campus sexual assault allegations, OCR has also been vigorously investigating complaints that dozens of universities violated Title IX in the past by failing to punish students alleged to have committed sexual assault. In some instances, OCR has required universities to reopen cases that universities previously found meritless. The message that universities are taking from this is that if they want to avoid the wrath of OCR and keep their federal funding, accused students need to be punished regardless of guilt.

In response to OCR pressure, some college administrators have allowed radical campus activists to seize control of the disciplinary process. In one case, a faculty member at Occidental College, Danielle Dirks, counseled a student who had consented to sex—she had asked the man in advance by text message if he had a condom, and told her friends she was planning to have sex with him—but was intoxicated at the time (as was her purported assailant), to file a complaint accusing the student of rape. To overcome the student's reluctance to file charges, Dirks told her that the man "fit the profile of other rapists on campus in that he had a high GPA in high school, was his class valedictorian, was on [a sports] team, and was from a good family."[16]

At Yale, meanwhile, the Title IX coordinator proudly reported that she was investigating a pending case resulting from a report provided by a third party that a male student sexually assaulted more than one female student. The party who made the allegation refused to identify the purported victims, nor did they step forward on their own. So, as Professor KC Johnson points out, "a Yale student is now being investigated as a serial rapist, with the possibility of sanctions—even though none of the females he allegedly raped have filed a complaint, or have even been identified. How any student could defend himself against such a charge is unclear."[17]

The OCR-dictated decline in procedural protections for accused students, combined with the empowerment of the forces on campus most dismissive of the rights of such students, and the widespread notion that OCR wants the disciplinary process to be biased in favor of accusers, has led to a witch hunt–like atmosphere on some campuses. Universities, especially those singled out for allegedly mishandling sex assault allegations in the past, are looking to make an example of someone, to prove their mettle to OCR.

For example, after OCR launched an investigation of how Swarthmore handles sexual assault cases, the college reopened a case against a male student that had previously been investigated and had resulted in no charges. After kangaroo-court proceedings that would make a wallaby blush, Swarthmore expelled the student. The student filed a lawsuit that detailed irregularities in and the lack of objectivity of the disciplinary proceeding that led to his expulsion. The college, chastened, and likely destined to lose at trial, agreed to vacate its findings and sanctions. As part of the settlement, Swarthmore acknowledged that the campus disciplinary process had treated the student unfairly.[18]

Another likely victim of a college's overzealousness to satisfy OCR was Dezmine Wells, a star basketball player at Xavier University. After a fellow student accused him of rape, a prosecutor empaneled a grand jury that refused to indict him. This indicates a weak case because, as the saying in legal circles goes, a grand jury will indict a ham sandwich. A Xavier disciplinary board nevertheless found Wells guilty of sexual assault and he was expelled from the university. Wells sued Xavier, claiming that the university, which OCR had previously investigated for Title IX violations, decided to scapegoat him to prove to OCR that it had changed its ways. A federal district court declined the university's motion to dismiss, pointing out that Wells's complaint enumerated substantial flaws in the proceedings that led to his expulsion.[19] Wells and the university soon reached a confidential settlement. This suggests at the very least that Xavier did not think it could easily defend its actions in further legal proceedings.[20]

In fact, by sparking an atmosphere on campuses that would please the poobahs of seventeenth-century Salem, Massachusetts, OCR's rules have resulted in the expulsion of dozens of students on dubious bases. This in turn has led to a countertrend of the penalized students using Title IX to sue the universities that punished them. These students argue that the university discriminated against them based on sex by presuming their guilt or otherwise skewing the process against them because they are men.[21]

The plaintiffs are undoubtedly right that on some campuses men are being treated unequally. Some universities, for example, operate from the premise that a man who has sex with an intoxicated female student is inherently guilty of sexual assault, even if she was a fully alert and enthusiastic participant in the encounter. A woman, however, faces no liability for having sex with an intoxicated male student. A Duke University dean, for example, was asked in a deposition how the university would judge a sexual assault allegation if both students were drunk. Presumably, suggested the lawyers, "they have raped each other and are subject to expulsion." The dean responded, "Assuming it is a male and female, it is the responsibility in the case of the male to gain consent before proceeding with sex."[22] So far, courts have been allowing most of the lawsuits by men claiming unjust proceedings to go forward, based not only on Title IX but also on grounds of breach of contract and violations of due process rights.

Meanwhile, the OCR guidance that has sparked all this is almost certainly illegal and unconstitutional, though no court has yet had an opportunity to rule on that issue. Title IX likely does not give OCR the authority to dictate the nature of university disciplinary proceedings. No cases suggest that an investigation of an allegation of sexual assault on campus must adhere to anything like the guidelines OCR is imposing on colleges.[23] The Supreme Court itself has stated in the context of Title IX that at least when university officials are sued for allegedly not properly intervening in student-on-student harassment "courts should refrain from second guessing the disciplinary decisions made by school administrators." School officials "must merely respond to known peer harassment in a manner that is not clearly unreasonable."[24]

Even if Title IX does give OCR the power to dictate campus disciplinary rules, OCR needed to go through the normal notice-and-comment regulatory process before making new regulations, rather than just announcing them through a "Dear Colleague" letter that is subject to neither normal administrative safeguards nor to judicial review.[25] Finally, even if OCR had followed proper procedures, the content of the letter likely violates the Due Process Clause of the Constitution by requiring universities to deprive their students of ordinary due process considerations when putting an important right, their right to pursue and finish their college education, in jeopardy. Courts have consistently held that the government acts illegally when it forces a private institution to treat an individual in a way that would be illegal if the government did it directly.[26]

No court in the United States would consider the procedures dictated by OCR consistent with due process for a defendant in a civil or criminal trial. Things get a bit fuzzy, because students typically are not entitled to full due process rights when being disciplined by government-run schools. Nevertheless, OCR cannot simply impose whatever standards it wants. In contrast to the OCR guidance, for example, at least one court has held that in the context of a disciplinary hearing at a state university, an accused student has a due process right to cross-examine his accuser when the outcome turns on the accuser's credibility, even when the hearing involves a sensitive subject like an accusation of sexual assault.[27]

Fresh from its illicit crusade against an imaginary sexual assault epidemic, OCR next sought to impose a draconian nationwide speech code at American universities. The first wave of university speech codes appeared in the late 1980s, with the rise of censorious political correctness. Courts did not treat public universities that adopted these speech codes kindly: federal courts overturned on First Amendment grounds codes at the University of Michigan, the University of Wisconsin, and Central Michigan University.[28] While private universities are exempt from the First Amendment, which only prohibits the government from censoring speech, most secular private schools have traditionally adopted the same free speech policies as public universities.

University speech codes seemed to be on life support until the federal Department of Education revived them in 1994. Male students at Santa Rosa Community College had posted anatomically explicit and sexually derogatory remarks about two female students on a discussion group hosted by the college's computer network.[29] Several students filed a complaint against the college with OCR. OCR found that the messages probably created a hostile educational environment on the basis of sex for one of the students. Toleration of such offensive speech by a university, the government added, would violate Title IX. To avoid losing federal funds, OCR announced, universities must proactively ban offensive speech by students and diligently punish any violations of that ban.

OCR's rule was dealt several crushing blows. First, in *Davis v. Monroe County Board of Education* in 1999, the Supreme Court ruled that to constitute illegal sexual harassment in education, sexual advances or other verbal or physical conduct must be severe and pervasive, create a hostile environment, and be "objectively offensive" to a "reasonable person."[30] The Clinton administration soon clarified that OCR's regulations must be interpreted as consistent with Supreme Court precedent. In 2003 the Bush administration OCR emphasized that illegal harassment "must include something beyond the mere expression of views . . . that some person finds offensive. . . . The Office for Civil Rights standards require that the conduct be evaluated from the perspective of a reasonable person." The letter also noted that because OCR was part of the government, OCR could not order private universities to adopt speech codes inconsistent with the First Amendment. OCR regulations, therefore, "should not be interpreted in ways that would lead to the suppression of [First Amendment] protected speech on public or private campuses."[31]

Many universities, public and private, nevertheless voluntarily continued to enforce harassment rules that amounted to stringent speech codes. Other universities, however, declined to enforce speech codes, either because their leaders believed that universities should be free marketplaces of ideas, or because they feared First Amendment lawsuits or bad publicity from organizations dedicated to freedom of speech on campus, in particular the Foundation for Individual Rights in Education (FIRE).

Fast forward to May 2013. OCR and the Justice Department jointly sent a letter to the University of Montana memorializing a settlement to a sexual harassment case brought against the university. The letter stated that it was intended to "serve as a blueprint for colleges and universities throughout the country." Ignoring Supreme Court precedent, the First Amendment, and OCR's own previous guidance, the letter declares that "sexual harassment should be more broadly defined as 'any unwelcome conduct of a sexual nature,'" including "verbal conduct," regardless of whether it is objectively offensive or sufficiently severe or pervasive to create a hostile environment.[32]

As FIRE pointed out in a blistering critique, this meant that the federal government was trying to impose a breathtakingly broad nationwide university speech code "that makes virtually every student in the United States a harasser." OCR was trying to force universities to ban "any expression related to sexual topics that offends any person." So, for example, universities would be required to punish a student for telling a "sexually themed joke overheard by any person who finds that joke offensive for any reason," or for "any request for dates or any flirtation that is not welcomed by the recipient of such a request or flirtation."[33]

Fortunately, a few months later, OCR got a new leader, Catherine Lhamon. Lhamon wrote in a letter to FIRE that "the agreement in the Montana case represents the resolution of that particular case and not OCR or DOJ policy." She also reiterated that OCR's understanding of hostile environment harassment in educational settings is "consistent" with the Supreme Court's definition.[34]

OCR even allowed the University of Montana to disregard some of the requirements of the agreement. But despite FIRE's urging, OCR failed to issue any clarification of the Dear Colleague letter it had sent to the thousands of colleges and universities it monitors. Some of these schools, not surprisingly, took the Dear Colleague letter at its word, as representing a blueprint for all college campuses. These schools amended their disciplinary policies to be consistent with the Dear Colleague letter's definition of sexual harassment, rather than with Supreme Court precedent, past OCR statements, and the letter OCR sent to FIRE.[35]

Meanwhile, in early 2014 the Departments of Justice and Education issued guidelines pressuring public school districts to adopt racial quotas when disciplining children. The basis for this guidance was studies showing that black children were over three times more likely to face serious punishment—suspension or expulsion—for misbehaving at school. The government concluded that school districts were engaging in massive illegal discrimination against black students.

In fact, however, the government had no basis for its conclusion.[36] The Supreme Court has explicitly stated that racial disparities in punishment do not by themselves prove discrimination, as they may just be consistent with the underlying rates of misbehavior by each group. There are no valid statistics (and the government hasn't cited any) from which one can infer that black students and white students would be expected to engage in serious misbehavior in school at the same rate.[37]

Unless there is some reason to expect kids to behave completely differently at school than outside of it, the school discipline figures are in line with what one would expect. African-American minors are arrested outside of school for violent crime at a rate approximately 3.5 times their share of the population.[38] Moreover, as former Department of Education attorney Hans Bader notes, the government's own statistics show that white boys were over two times as likely to be suspended as their peers of Asian descent. By the government's logic, this means, absurdly, that school districts must be discriminating against white students and in favor of Asians.[39] As of this writing, Minneapolis education authorities have announced their intention to end the black/white gap in suspensions and expulsions, a plan that struck many observers as announcing the imposition of quotas on school discipline.[40]

The Obama administration's attempts to unreasonably stretch antidiscrimination law also led the Equal Employment Opportunity Commission to try to force employers to ignore job applicants' criminal records. The theory, rejected so far by the courts, is that requiring a clean record both imposes a disproportionate burden on minority applicants, and is only tangentially relevant to many jobs.

Nobody sensible wants to inhibit released prisoners from successfully reintegrating into society. But that doesn't turn an employer understandably wary of hiring ex-cons into a practitioner of illegal racial discrimination. The last time the EEOC tried to punish companies for using background checks, two decades ago, federal judge Jose Alejandro Gonzalez Jr. wrote that equating suspicion of convicted criminals with discrimination against minorities "is an insult to millions of honest [members of minority groups]. Obviously a rule refusing honest employment to convicted applicants is going to have a disparate impact upon thieves."[41]

Enforcement of antidiscrimination laws represents a good test of the Obama administration's commitment to the Constitution and the rule of law. In many cases, core Democratic constituencies—feminists, liberal activists, organizations representing minority groups, and others—seek to push policy in one direction, while constitutional and legal niceties dictate the opposite. Unfortunately, the Obama administration seems to have stacked relevant federal enforcement agencies with left-wing ideologues who have invested their resources in the various dubious endeavors described in this chapter, the Constitution and the rule of law be damned.

CONCLUSION

THOSE WHO CRITICIZE the Obama administration's lawlessness are often dismissed by administration partisans as "wingnuts" or other varieties of kook, but one hardly needs to be a tinfoil-hat wearer to detect a troubling pattern of misbehavior by the administration. This book has focused on Obama administration actions that have been illegal or unconstitutional based on mainstream, widely accepted understandings of the law. Indeed, many of the administration's actions detailed here were illegal or unconstitutional based on what President Obama himself said during his 2008 election campaign about constitutional limits on presidential power. And the Obama administration has lost several major Supreme Court cases 9–0, failing to attract even the votes of Obama's own liberal appointees.

When I started researching this book I anticipated that I would argue that President Obama has continued a long-standing trend of the abuse of executive power, despite his promises to reverse this trend. As I delved into the administration's record, however, I became convinced that the administration's lawlessness has well exceeded that of its recent predecessors, certainly in degree, but also in kind.

Presidential administrations from Ford to Bush II all had their moments when the president and his underlings overstepped legal boundaries—for example, the Iran-Contra scandal in the Reagan Administration, war without congressional authorization and in violation of the War Powers Resolution in Bosnia in the Clinton administration, domestic surveillance by the National Security Agency without statutory authority in the Bush II administration—but none of those administrations were so persistent in their abuses, across such a wide range of both domestic and foreign affairs, as the Obama administration has been.

As my research progressed, as a law professor I grew increasingly concerned, and as an American, increasingly angry. And I'm not the only one. Broken promises, lawless behavior, and secretive presidential actions have combined to set public faith in government at an all-time low—worse even than in the aftermath of the Vietnam War and Nixon's Watergate. This is quite an achievement for an administration that many thought would restore Americans' faith in the federal government.

But what can be done? It's too late for the Obama administration to reverse most of its misdeeds, but it can still reverse or mitigate some of them. It can make a point of adhering to the War Powers Resolution when taking further military action. It can begin cooperating with Congress on oversight hearings. It can launch a serious investigation of the IRS's illegal targeting of conservative groups. And it can revoke the illegal Department of Education rules for adjudicating sexual assault allegations that are causing a witch-hunt-like environment on college campuses.

Meanwhile, the House and Senate should launch bipartisan investigations of the Obama administration's unconstitutional actions, with an eye toward setting ground rules for the next president, enforced by legislation whenever possible. Because no one knows whether that president will be a Republican or Democrat, new laws that will apply to the next administration will have extra credibility as nonpartisan reforms. The problem is that President Obama is likely to veto any legislation that could be seen as a rebuke to his legacy.

Courts, meanwhile, have managed to restrain some lawless behavior by presidents, including some described in this book. In the future, they should interpret "standing" rules more liberally, which would allow a wider range of challenges to the abuse of presidential authority. The Supreme Court has been reluctant to liberalize standing to sue the president because the framers of the Constitution believed that Congress, and not the courts, should be the primary check on presidential abuses. The Supreme Court should now acknowledge that the Constitution's visionaries were wrong. They failed to anticipate the emergence of the two-party system, which makes it virtually impossible for Congress to rein in a sitting president because members of the president's party run interference for him. And they failed to envision the political and economic developments that shifted the fulcrum of power from Congress, where it was intended to be, to the president.

Congress's ultimate check on presidential abuses, the power to remove the president through impeachment and conviction, is virtually toothless because it requires a majority vote of the House of Representatives to impeach, and two-thirds of the Senate to convict. Absent Nixon-level lawbreaking, in practice this means impeachment is a serious threat only when the president is of one party, and the House and Senate are controlled by the other, with a two-thirds majority in the latter. That has occurred only one time in American history, one hundred and fifty years ago—and it led to the impeachment and near-conviction of President Andrew Johnson. More recently, President Bill Clinton was impeached, but not convicted, leading to a backlash against the Republican Party for, among other things, wasting everyone's time and energy on what seemed to many like a futile quest for vengeance.

The next president can take measures to restore the rule of law, including respecting the legal advice of the Office of Legal Counsel even when it conflicts with short-term political priorities. The OLC is an imperfect check on presidential abuses, and indeed as a part of the executive branch of government it tends to interpret the president's powers too expansively. Nevertheless, it is a somewhat independent voice within presidential administrations otherwise staffed by sycophants and political operators whose job descriptions emphatically do not include respecting the rule of law. The OLC's tendency to bend over backward to favor presidential authority is all the more reason it should be heeded when it hoists a red flag.

And because the OLC is inclined to justify exercises of presidential power, its major legal memoranda should be published when issued. This way, the public can judge the legal basis for controversial presidential actions. This was *not* done, for example, with the OLC's justification for President Obama's claim that the War Powers Resolution did not apply to American intervention in the Libyan civil war. Yale law professor Bruce Ackerman writes, "I had expected our law professor-president to bring the [OLC] back to its origins as a serious guardian of legality within the executive branch. He has failed."[1] What Ackerman calls the Obama administration's "politically-inspired manipulation" of the OLC sorely needs to be reversed by the next president. Moreover, the next president should consider appointing some OLC lawyers from the other party to help ensure partisan blinders are not affecting the OLC's legal conclusions.

The next president may even find it politically expedient to prioritize adherence to the Constitution and the protection of the rule of law. Despite short-term political gains, both President Obama and President George W. Bush ultimately suffered in the polls thanks to a perception that their administrations had behaved lawlessly.

Ultimately, though, we cannot assume that the next president, Republican or Democrat, will improve matters. The historical trend has been for new presidents, of whichever party, to institutionalize whatever constitutional abuses their predecessors engaged in, and then seek even more power. President Obama ran strongly against Bush administration excesses, and likely sincerely expected to reverse them. Once in office, however, Obama institutionalized many of the policies and practices he had previously denounced as unlawful, and then did further damage to the Constitution and the rule of law.

One can only hope for future presidents with the virtue to exercise self-restraint, willing to voluntarily limit their own exercise of power even when pressing political considerations dictate otherwise. This virtue that has been especially lacking in the Obama administration, for reasons described in chapter 1.

Self-restraint is especially important because even a president willing to stick to the letter of the law can still abuse his power. In addition to the various blatantly illegal actions taken by the Obama administration and detailed in this book, President Obama has also done things that arguably are technically legal, but have undermined the public's faith in the government and the rule of law, and are contrary to the norms of our legal system that have been widely respected since the nation's founding.

For example, the National Security Agency, which reports to the president, collected huge amounts of data on American citizens living in the United States without public debate and with scant oversight from the president. President Obama only seemed to pay attention to the issue when revelations by whistleblower Edward Snowden and the associated public backlash forced him to. NSA spying on Americans arguably violates the Constitution's Fourth Amendment, but most courts have so far sided with the government. Contrary to some critics, then, it would be difficult to argue that the NSA's actions were clearly illegal.

With courts AWOL, Congress has the authority to ensure that NSA spying stays within appropriate bounds. Yet, when Director of National Intelligence James Clapper lied to the Senate when asked if the government collects "any type of data at all on millions or hundreds of millions of Americans," he faced no consequences from the president. If presidential appointees can lie under oath with impunity, Congress cannot serve as a proper check on the agencies those appointees run.

President Obama has also acted improperly in granting temporary amnesty and work permits to millions of illegal immigrants. Congress and the president failed to come to an agreement to pass the "Dream Act," a bill that would have allowed individuals brought to the United States as children to have a path to citizenship subject to various conditions. President Obama, feeling pressure from pro-immigration activist supporters, essentially enacted most of the provisions of the Dream Act by executive order, for overtly political reasons. This happened only months after he publicly stated, "Believe me, the idea of doing things on my own is very tempting. I promise you. Not just on immigration reform. But that's not how our system works. That's not how our democracy functions. That's not how our Constitution is written."[2] He was right the first time.

After the 2014 midterm elections made it clear that Obama would have to get immigration reform through a Republican Congress, Obama acted unilaterally once again, granting millions of undocumented residents of the United States de facto legal status and permission to work legally. Many critics argued that Obama's actions had no legal basis. Obama's defenders pointed both to the general notion of the president's discretion to reallocate prosecutorial resources and also to obscure provisions of the immigration statutes—provisions that Obama originally did not cite in justifying his actions—that give the president authority to decline to deport people. The immigration laws also allow those whose deportation is delayed indefinitely to receive work permits.[3] Obama's allies pointed out that other presidents had used these powers without much controversy, usually in emergency circumstances, as when tens of thousands of Cubans fled Castro's communist revolution.

Even if one concludes that there is at least a plausible legal defense of Obama's immigration unilateralism, no president had ever used the discretion provided by immigration laws and inherent to his office simply to evade congressional opposition to his policies, nor to extend de facto legal status to so many people. It corrodes public respect for the legal system when the president uses loopholes to evade the normal legislative process and enact an extremely controversial, wide-ranging policy that Congress has declined to endorse.

Obama's unilateralism, moreover, sets a dangerous precedent by concentrating so much power in the president. Several liberal commentators have expressed concern that Obama's immigration actions portend a future in which presidents effectively dismantle parts of the regulatory state through nonenforcement.[4] Cornell law professor Michael Dorf, for example, worries that Obama violated a norm that constrains abuse of presidential discretion, which is that a "president may not use considerations of resource allocation merely as a pretext for undermining a law that he would prefer to simply not enforce regardless of resources."[5] And if President Obama can do this with regard to immigration, in seeming violation of his constitutional duty to take care that the laws be faithfully executed, what's to stop future presidents, including conservative Republican presidents, from using similar tactics?[6]

Finally, Obama acted improperly in forcing states to adopt so-called Common Core standards in their public schools. The No Child Left Behind law, a bipartisan law sponsored by Senator Ted Kennedy and signed by President George W. Bush, required public schools to meet draconian federal achievement goals. States where schools failed to meet these goals stood to lose a huge amount of federal funding unless the Department of Education granted them waivers. The Obama administration agreed to give states waivers—but only if the states adopted curricula that met Common Core standards. Adopting these standards would also make them eligible for additional federal "Race to the Top" funds.[7]

Nothing in No Child Left Behind explicitly prohibited the administration from conditioning the waivers on adoption of particular standards, like Common Core. Nevertheless, it was highly improper for the administration to use the law to impose controversial new national educational standards, applicable to the vast majority of schools throughout the United States, all done through the bureaucracy without any change to the law and without giving Congress any say.

In other words, even a president who is acting within the letter of the law, or who at least can make a plausible case that he is doing so, may behave in ways that undermine the Constitution, the rule of law, and public faith in our legislative system. As liberal writer Jonathan Chait puts it, "Our Constitution and legal structure alone don't secure the Republic. We also depend on norms—or an implied understanding of what sort of behavior is acceptable."[8] What's needed is a president with the humility to recognize that his own immediate political interests and policy goals, his own pursuit and exercise of power, are and must be subordinate to the greater long-term public interest in preserving the Constitution and the rule of law.

It's a daunting challenge to find people with the self-confidence to successfully pursue the presidency, but the foresight and humility to recognize that their presidency is just a blip in a much longer American story, and to recognize that they should therefore strive to preserve our constitutional system even when it creates short-term political costs. We can take some inspiration from our first president, George Washington. Washington twice resigned from office rather than cling to political power. First, when the Revolutionary War ended, instead of seeking the dictatorial power many wanted to bestow on him, he resigned from the military and returned to his Mount Vernon plantation. After being drafted as the nation's first president and serving two terms, he declined to run again, depriving himself of almost-certain victory. Washington's willingness to voluntarily turn over the reins of power marked the first peaceful democratic transition in the Western world since the heyday of the Roman Empire. His voluntary term limit set a precedent that lasted until Franklin Roosevelt sought a third term in office on the cusp of World War II in 1940.

Washington, in short, was willing to limit his own power for the sake of setting a precedent that the nation's welfare is more important than personal ambition and short-term politics. Restoring presidential respect for the Constitution and the rule of law may require finding a twenty-first-century president who, emphatically unlike Barack Obama, has similar virtues.

ACKNOWLEDGMENTS

Thank you to Lillian Bernstein, Stanley Bernstein, Ilya Shapiro, and Ilya Somin for reading and commenting on complete draft manuscripts of this book. Josh Blackman, Gene Healy, Karen Horwitz, Nelson Lund, John McGinnis, Chris Newman, Aaron Saiger, Brad Smith, and Todd Zywicki provided helpful comments on one or more chapters. Hans Bader, Charles Barzun, Yehoshua Bedrick, Michael Cannon, and KC Johnson provided useful leads and advice on specific issues the book addresses.

Much of Chapter 1, in an earlier incarnation, appeared in the October 2014 issue of *Commentary*.

Sigal Bernstein amicably tolerated my occasional pessimistic pronouncements early in the book-writing process, such as "I'm never going to finish this book," and my fatigue-induced grouchiness on days after writing momentum kept me typing away until three A.M.

Special thanks go to my children. I promise to start doing with all of you all the things I promised to do "when Daddy finishes writing his book."

DAVID E. BERNSTEIN
Arlington, Virginia

NOTES

Foreword

1. Ezra Klein, "Obama's Gift," *American Prospect*, January 4, 2008, http://prospect.org/article/obamas-gift.
2. Mark Morford, "Is Obama an Enlightened Being? / Spiritual Wise Ones Say: This Sure Ain't No Ordinary Politician. You Buying It?," *SFGate*, June 6, 2008, http://www.sfgate.com/entertainment/morford/article/Is-Obama-an-enlightened-being-Spiritual-wise-2544395.php; emphasis in original.
3. Michelle Obama, speech at the University of California, Los Angeles, on February 1, 2008. Transcription at *Hamilton, Madison, and Jay* (blog), February 15, 2008, http://fedpapers.blogspot.com/2008/02/michelle-obamas-speech-ucla-two-weeks.html.
4. Nancy Gibbs, "How Obama Rewrote the Book," *Time*, November 5, 2008, www.time.com/time/magazine/article/0,9171,1856982,00.html.
5. "Senator Obama's Announcement," *New York Times*, February 10, 2007, http://www.nytimes.com/2007/02/10/us/politics/11obama-text.html?pagewanted=print.
6. "Barack Obama's March 4 Speech," transcript, *New York Times*, March 4, 2008, http://www.nytimes.com/2008/03/04/us/politics/04text-obama.html?pagewanted=all&_r=1&.
7. James Hohmann and John F. Harris, "10 Quotes That Haunt Obama," *Politico*, October 2, 2012, http://www.politico.com/story/2012/10/10-quotes-that-haunt-obama-081895.
8. Barack Obama, Remarks in Columbia, Missouri, October 30, 2008,

http://www.presidency.ucsb.edu/ws/index.php?pid=84665&stı=#axz
zılvulJr36.

9. "Obama's Nomination Victory Speech in St. Paul," *Huffington Post*, November 5, 2008, http://www.huffingtonpost.com/2008/06/03/obamas
-nomination-victory_n_105028.html.

10. "President Barack Obama's Inaugural Address," White House, January 21, 2009, https://www.whitehouse.gov/blog/2009/01/21/president
-barack-obamas-inaugural-address.

11. See Angie Drobnic Holan, "Lie of the Year: 'If You Like Your Health Care Plan, You Can Keep It,'" *Tampa Bay Times*, PolitiFact.com, December 12, 2013, http://www.politifact.com/truth-o-meter/article/2013
/dec/12/lie-year-if-you-like-your-health-care-plan-keep-it/.

12. See "Obama's McCain Smackdown: Stop Campaigning, Election's Over," *FoxNews.com*, February 25, 2010, http://www.foxnews.com
/politics/2010/02/25/obamas-mccain-smackdown-stop-campaigning
-elections/.

13. See "Abuse of Power," *Wall Street Journal*, March 3, 2010, http://www
.wsj.com/articles/SB10001424052748704625004575089362731862750.

14. "Transparency and Open Government: Memorandum for the Heads of Executive Departments and Agencies," White House, January 21, 2009, https://www.whitehouse.gov/the_press_office/Transparencyand
OpenGovernment.

15. "President Obama Delivers Remarks at Swearing-In Ceremony," January 21, 2009, http://www.fas.org/sgp/news/2009/01/obama012109
.html.

16. Jonathan Easley, "Obama Says His Is 'Most Transparent Administration' Ever," Briefing Room (blog), *The Hill*, February 14, 2013, http://thehill
.com/blogs/blog-briefing-room/news/283335-obama-this-is-the-most
-transparent-administration-in-history.

17. "President Obama Delivers Remarks at Swearing-In Ceremony."

18. Mark Tapscott, "'Most Transparent' White House Ever Rewrote the FOIA to Suppress Politically Sensitive Docs," *Washington Examiner*, September 8, 2015, http://www.washingtonexaminer.com/most-trans
parent-white-house-ever-rewrote-the-foia-to-suppress-politically-sensi
tive-docs/article/2545824.

19. Ibid.

20. John Diaz, "Obama Failing to Run 'Most Transparent' Administration," *San Francisco Chronicle*, April 25, 2015, http://www.sfchronicle.com

/ opinion / diaz / article / Obama-failing-to-run-most-transparent
-6222936.php.

21. Conor Friedersdorf, "The Obama Administration's Abject Failure on Transparency," *The Atlantic*, February 2, 2012, http:// www.theatlantic .com / politics / archive / 2012 / 02 / the-obama-administrations-abject-fail ure-on-transparency / 252387 / #disqus_thread.

22. Jason Ross Arnold, "Has Obama Delivered the 'Most Transparent' Administration in History?," Monkey Cage (blog), *Washington Post*, March 16, 2015, http:// www.washingtonpost.com / blogs / monkey-cage / wp / 2015 / 03 / 16 / has-obama-delivered-the-most-transparent-administra tion-in-history /; emphasis added.

23. "Vowing Transparency, Obama OKs Ethics Guidelines," CNN, January 21, 2009, http:// www.cnn.com / 2009 / POLITICS / 01 / 21 / obama.busi ness / index.html.

24. From 2013 to 2014, I served as the Ranking Member on the Constitution Subcommittee of the Senate Judiciary Committee, and in that capacity, I released a report chronicling *76 different lawless acts* by the Obama administration. See "Sen. Cruz Releases Fourth Report on Obama Administration's Lawlessness," U.S. Senator for Texas: Ted Cruz, press release, May 7, 2014, http:// www.cruz.senate.gov / ?p=press_release&id=1218.

25. Ted Cruz, "The Obama Administration's Unprecedented Lawlessness," *Harvard Journal of Law and Public Policy* 38 (February 2015): 100–111, http:// www.harvard-jlpp.com / wp-content / uploads / 2015 / 02 / Cruz _Final.pdf.

26. Ibid., 111–14.

27. See National Labor Relations Board v. Noel Canning, 134 S. Ct. 2550 (2014).

28. Ronald J. Pestritto, "The Progressive Rejection of the Founding," introduction to *The U.S. Constitution: A Reader* (Hillsdale, MI: Hillsdale College Press, 2012), 617.

29. Ibid., 617–18.

30. Woodrow Wilson, *Congressional Government: A Study in American Politics* (Baltimore, MD: Johns Hopkins University Press, 1981; first published in 1885), 215.

31. Ibid. (emphasis added).

32. Woodrow Wilson, *Constitutional Government in the United States* (New York: Columbia University Press, 1908), 56.

33. Ibid.

34. Ibid., 57; see also Charles R. Kesler, *I Am the Change: Barack Obama and the Crisis of Liberalism* (New York: Broadside Books, 2012), 75.

35. See Wilson, *Constitutional Government*, 56–57; Kesler, *I Am the Change*, 75.

36. Barack Obama, *The Audacity of Hope: Thoughts on Reclaiming the American Dream* (New York: Crown, 2006), 90.

37. White House Office of the Press Secretary, "Inaugural Address by President Barack Obama," January 21, 2013, https://www.whitehouse.gov/the-press-office/2013/01/21/inaugural-address-president-barack-obama.

38. "Transcript of Obama Redistribution of Wealth Audio," *Free Republic* (website), October 26, 2008, http://www.freerepublic.com/focus/f-news/2116149/posts.

39. Nicholas Ballasy, "Obama Will Act for Unemployed Vets 'With or Without Congress,'" *Daily Caller* (website), November 7, 2011, http://dailycaller.com/2011/11/07/obama-will-act-for-unemployed-vets-with-or-without-congress-video/.

40. "Obama: If Congress Won't Act I Will," Associated Press, October 31, 2011, available at *Newsday*, http://www.newsday.com/news/nation/obama-if-congress-won-t-act-i-will-1.3287261.

41. Ryan Grim, "State of the Union Speech Promises Climate Change Executive Action," *Huffington Post*, February 13, 2013, http://www.huffingtonpost.com/2013/02/13/state-of-the-union_n_2673983.html.

42. White House Office of the Press Secretary, "Weekly Address: Working When Congress Won't Act," May 17, 2014, https://www.whitehouse.gov/the-press-office/2014/05/17/weekly-address-working-when-congress-won-t-act.

43. "Transcript of President Barack Obama with Univision," *Los Angeles Times*, October 25, 2010, http://latimesblogs.latimes.com/washington/2010/10/transcript-of-president-barack-obama-with-univision.html.

44. Anita Kumar, "Obama Vows to Act on Issues If Congress Won't," *McClatchyDC* (website), August 6, 2014, http://www.mcclatchydc.com/news/politics-government/white-house/article24771547.html.

45. Anthony Everitt, *Cicero: The Life and Times of Rome's Greatest Politician* (New York: Random House, 2003), 321–22.

46. "Authorization to Initiate Litigation for the Actions by the President Inconsistent with His Duties under the Constitution of the United States" (written statement of Jonathan Turley, George Washington University), hearing before the House Rules Committee, 113th Con-

gress (July 16, 2014), available at http://docs.house.gov/meetings/RU
/RU00/20140716/102507/HMTG-113-RU00-Wstate-TurleyJ-20140716.pdf.

47. Greg Richter, "Jonathan Turley: America Becoming 'Imperial Presidency,'" *Newsmax* (website), June 4, 2014, http://www.newsmax.com
/Newsfront/Jonathan-Turley-Obama-presidency-power/2014/06/04
/id/575014/.

48. Jonathan Turley, "Nixon Has Won Watergate," *USA Today*, March 26,
2013, http://www.usatoday.com/story/opinion/2013/03/25/nixon-has
-won-watergate/2019443/.

Introduction

1. "[FLASHBACK] In 2008 Candidate Obama Said He Would Not Use
Signing Statements to Go Around Congress," YouTube video, 1:39,
from a campaign event in Billings, Montana, on May 19, 2008, posted
by "LSUDVM," June 5, 2014, https://www.youtube.com/watch?v=oN
dxanhbzDQ.

2. "Obama in 2007: No More Spying on Citizens Who Are Not Suspected
of a Crime," YouTube video, 1:05, from a speech at the Woodrow Wilson Center in August 2007, posted by John Sexton, June 6, 2013, https://
www.youtube.com/watch?v=WAQlsS9diBs.

3. Onan Coca, "Viral Video of Obama in 2008 Implying Executive Orders
Are Unconstitutional," *Eagle Rising* (website), February 15, 2014, http://
eaglerising.com/4692/viral-video-obama-2008-implying-executive-
orders-unconstitutional.

4. Jeffrey Rosen, "Card Carrying," *New Republic*, February 27, 2008, http://
www.newrepublic.com/article/card-carrying.

5. Ibid.

6. Peter Finn and Anne E. Kornblut, "Guantanamo Bay: How the White
House Lost the Fight to Close It," *Washington Post*, April 23, 2011, http://
www.washingtonpost.com/world/guantanamo-bay-how-the-white-
house-lost-the-fight-to-close-it/2011/04/14/AFtxR5XE_story.html.

7. Barack Obama, Remarks by the President on the Economy and Housing,
October 24, 2011, http://www.whitehouse.gov/the-press-office/2011/10
/24/remarks-president-economy-and-housing.

8. Barack Obama, Remarks by the President on the Economy, July 25, 2013,
http://www.whitehouse.gov/the-press-office/2013/07/25/remarks
-president-economy-jacksonville-fl.

9. Barack Obama, Remarks at the General Electric Company Gas Engines Plant in Waukesha, Wisconsin, January 30, 2014, http://www.gpo.gov/fdsys/pkg/DCPD-201400055/html/DCPD-201400055.htm.

10. Barack Obama, Remarks by the President on No Child Left Behind Flexibility, February 9, 2012, http://www.whitehouse.gov/the-press-office/2012/02/09/remarks-president-no-child-left-behind-flexibility.

11. Jonathan Turley, "Obama's Irresponsible Taunt," *New York Daily News*, July 6, 2014, http://www.nydailynews.com/opinion/obama-irresponsible-taunt-article-1.1854252#ixzz36pFC7O7j.

12. Eli Lake, "Obama Uses Bush Plan for Terror War," *Washington Times*, September 9, 2010, http://www.washingtontimes.com/news/2010/sep/9/obama-uses-bush-plan-for-terror-war/?page=all.

13. Jeffrey Rosen, "The President Should Finally Fight for Civil Liberties," *New Republic*, March 8, 2012, http://www.newrepublic.com/article/politics/101447/symposium-obama-civil-liberties-privacy.

Chapter 1: Why So Lawless?

1. See Gene Healy, *The Cult of the Presidency: America's Dangerous Devotion to Executive Power* (Washington, DC: Cato Institute, 2008); Charlie Savage, *The Return of the Imperial Presidency and the Subversion of American Democracy* (New York: Little Brown, 2007).

2. Jonathan Turley, "Obama's Irresponsible Taunt," *New York Daily News*, July 6, 2014, http://www.nydailynews.com/opinion/obama-irresponsible-taunt-article-1.1854252#ixzz36pFC7O7j.

3. Josh Blackman, "Gridlock and Executive Power," *Social Science Research Network* (website), July 14, 2014, http://papers.ssrn.com/sol3/papers.cfm?abstract_id=2466707; Josh Blackman, "We Can't Wait," *Josh Blackman's Blog*, August 14, 2014, http://joshblackman.com/blog/2014/08/14/we-cant-wait.

4. American Constitution Society, Mission, https://www.acslaw.org/about/mission.

5. Brian Z. Tamanaha, *Law as a Means to an End: Threat to the Rule of Law* (New York: Cambridge University Press, 2006), 120–23.

6. Charles L. Barzun, "The Forgotten Foundations of Hart and Sacks," *Virginia Law Review* 99: 1 (2013).

7. Quoted in Tamanaha, *Law as a Means to an End*, 121.

8. E.g., Catherine MacKinnon, *A Feminist Theory of the State* (Cambridge,

MA: Harvard University Press, 1989); Deborah Rhode, *Justice and Gender* (Cambridge, MA: Harvard University Press, 1989).

9. Daniel A. Farber and Suzanne Sherry, *Beyond All Reason: The Radical Assault on Truth in American Law* (New York: Oxford University Press, 1997), 118.

10. Mark Tushnet, "An Essay on Rights," *Texas Law Review* 62 (1984), 1363–64. See also Duncan Kennedy, "The Critique of Rights in Critical Legal Studies," in *Left Legalism/Left Critique*, eds. Wendy Brown and Janet Halley (Durham: Duke University Press, 2002), 178.

11. Josh Blackman, "We Can't Wait."

12. Josh Blackman, "Obama on Colbert," *Josh Blackman's Blog*, December 9, 2014, http://joshblackman.com/blog/2014/12/09/obama-on-colbert-theres-always-the-temptation-to-want-to-go-ahead-and-get-stuff-done-and-democracy-is-messy-and-its-complicated.

13. Turley, "Obama's Irresponsible Taunt."

14. Ibid.

15. Dylan Byers, "The Sharyl Attkisson Approach," *Politico*, May 24, 2013, http://www.politico.com/story/2013/05/sharyl-attkisson-91871.html.

16. Dylan Byers, "The Post's Sharyl Attkisson Piece," *Politico*, May 8, 2013, http://www.politico.com/blogs/media/2013/05/the-posts-sharyl-attkisson-piece-163496.html.

17. "Charges of Bad Journalism at CBS News," Reliable Sources, CNN, April 20, 2014, http://reliablesources.blogs.cnn.com/2014/04/20/charges-of-bad-journalism-at-cbs-news.

18. James Oliphant, "Progressive Bloggers Are Doing the White House's Job," *National Journal*, May 9, 2014, http://www.nationaljournal.com/magazine/progressive-bloggers-are-doing-the-white-house-s-job-20140509.

19. Ibid.; John Podhoretz, "Conservative Media Is Unintentionally Protecting Obama," *New York Post*, April 5, 2014, http://nypost.com/2014/04/05/rise-of-conservative-media-is-unintentionally-protecting-obama.

20. Quoted in Steven Schier, *Transforming America: Barack Obama in the White House* (New York: Rowan and Littlefield, 2011), 114.

21. Quoted in Jodi Kantor, *The Obamas* (New York: Little Brown, 2012), 66.

22. David French, "Obama, Critical Race Theory, and Harvard Law School," *National Review*, March 8, 2012, http://www.nationalreview.com/corner/292994/obama-critical-race-theory-and-harvard-law-school-david-french.

23. Jodi Kantor, "In Law School, Obama Found Political Voice," *New York Times*, January 28, 2007, http://www.nytimes.com/2007/01/28/us/politics/28obama.html.

24. See, e.g., Paul Kengor, *The Communist: Frank Marshall Davis, The Untold Story of Barack Obama's Mentor* (New York: Mercury Ink, 2012); Stanley Kurtz, *Radical in Chief* (New York: Threshold Editions, 2010); Barack Obama, *Dreams from My Father* (New York: Times Books, 1995).

25. Rebecca Shabad, "Obama Tells Donors: 'I'm Not a Particularly Ideological Person,'" Briefing Room (blog), *The Hill*, November 25, 2013, http://thehill.com/blogs/blog-briefing-room/news/191291-obama-im-not-a-particularly-ideological-person#ixzz38nDKRvVw.

26. Chuck Todd, *The Stranger* (New York: Little Brown, 2014).

27. Dinitia Smith, "No Regrets for a Love of Explosives; In a Memoir of Sorts, a War Protester Talks of Life with the Weathermen," *New York Times*, September 11, 2001, http://www.nytimes.com/2001/09/11/books/no-regrets-for-love-explosives-memoir-sorts-war-protester-talks-life-with.html.

28. "Transcript, Democratic Debate in Philadelphia," *New York Times*, April 16, 2008, http://www.nytimes.com/2008/04/16/us/politics/16text-debate.html?_r=2&oref=slogin&pagewanted=all&oref=slogin.

29. Gloria Borger, Kevin Bohn, and Brian Rokus, "Former Defense Secretary Lays Out Disagreements with President Obama," CNN, October 7, 2014, http://www.cnn.com/2014/10/07/politics/panetta-disagreements-obama-borger-interview.

Chapter 2: No Justice at the Justice Department

1. See Ilya Shapiro, "Why Obama Keeps Losing at the Supreme Court," *Bloomberg View*, June 6, 2013, http://www.bloombergview.com/articles/2013-06-06/why-obama-keeps-losing-at-the-supreme-court; Ilya Shapiro, "Why Obama Strikes Out in Court," *Wall Street Journal*, June 5, 2012, http://online.wsj.com/articles/SB10001424052702303918204577444221444859342.

2. Ed O'Keefe and Sari Horwitz, "House Votes to Hold Attorney General Eric Holder in Contempt," *Washington Post*, June 28, 2012, http://www.washingtonpost.com/politics/fast-and-furious-house-plans-vote-on-holding-eric-holder-in-contempt/2012/06/28/gJQAznlG9V_story.html.

3. Hans Bader, "Obama Administration Ignores Constitution and Politi- cizes Justice on D.C. 'Voting Rights' Bill," *Examiner.com*, April 15, 2009, http://web.archive.org/web/20121226032646/http://www.examiner .com/article/obama-administration-ignores-constitution-and-politi cizes-justice-on-d-c-voting-rights-bill.

4. Carrie Johnson, "Some in Justice Department See D.C. Vote in House as Unconstitutional," *Washington Post*, April 1, 2009, http://www.washing tonpost.com/wp-dyn/content/article/2009/03/31/AR2009033104426 .html.

5. John Fund and Hans von Spakovsy, *Obama's Enforcer: Eric Holder's Justice Department* (New York: Broadside Books, 2014), 47.

6. "Donald Berwick on Redistributing Wealth," YouTube video, 2:15, ex- cerpt from a 2008 speech to a British audience, posted by "btdome," https://www.youtube.com/watch?v=r2Kevz_9lsw.

7. Sarah Kliff, "Medicare Administrator Donald Berwick Resigns in the Face of Republican Opposition," *Washington Post*, November 23, 2011, http://www.washingtonpost.com/national/health-science/medicare -administrator-donald-berwick-resigns-in-the-face-of-republican-oppo sition/2011/11/23/gIQA5S7mpN_story.html.

8. "President Obama Announces Recess Appointments to Key Adminis- tration Posts," press release, January 4, 2012, http://www.whitehouse .gov/the-press-office/2012/01/04/president-obama-announces-recess -appointments-key-administration-posts.

9. Office of Legal Counsel, Lawfulness of Recess Appointments during a Recess of the Senate Notwithstanding Periodic Pro Forma Sessions, 36 Op. O.L.C. slip op. at 5 (January 6, 2012), http://www.justice.gov/olc /opiniondocs/pro-forma-sessions-opinion.pdf.

10. See, e.g., Gene Healy, *False Idol: Barack Obama and the Continuing Cult of the Presidency* (Washington, DC: Cato Institute, 2012), 50.

11. Fund and von Spakovsky, *Obama's Enforcer*, 47.

12. Jonathan Turley, "Obama's Irresponsible Taunt," *New York Daily News*, July 6, 2014, http://www.nydailynews.com/opinion/obama-irresponsible -taunt-article-1.1854252#ixzz36pFC7O7j.

13. Transcript of Oral Argument, NLRB v. Noel Canning, January 13, 2014, http://www.supremecourt.gov/oral_arguments/argument_transcripts /12-1281_d1o2.pdf.

14. Ibid.

15. NLRB v. Noel Canning, 134 S. Ct. 2550 (2014).

16. US Justice Department Office of the Inspector General and Office of Professional Responsibility, An Investigation of Allegations of Politicized Hiring in the Department of Justice Honors Program and Summer Law Intern Program, June 24, 2008, http://online.wsj.com/public/resources/documents/dojsummerlaw20080624.pdf.

17. US Department of Justice Office of the Inspector General, A Review of the Operations of the Voting Section of the Civil Rights Division (March 2013), 134, http://www.justice.gov/oig/reports/2013/s1303.pdf.

18. Ibid., 133.

19. Ibid., 134–35.

20. Charlie Savage, "Racial Motive Alleged in a Justice Dept. Decision," *New York Times*, July 6, 2010, http://www.nytimes.com/2010/07/07/us/07rights.html.

21. Abigail Thernstrom, "The New Black Panther Case: A Conservative Dissent," *National Review Online*, July 6, 2010, http://www.national review.com/articles/243408/new-black-panther-case-br-conservative-dissent-abigail-thernstrom.

22. Jerry Markon and Krissah Thompson, "Dispute over New Black Panthers Case Causes Deep Divisions," *Washington Post*, Oct. 22, 2009, http://www.washingtonpost.com/wp-dyn/content/article/2010/10/22/AR2010102203982.html; Judicial Watch, Inc. v. U.S. Dept. of Justice, 878 F. Supp. 2d 225 (D.D.C. 2012).

23. Charlie Savage, "For Holder, New Congress Means New Headaches," *New York Times*, December 30, 2010, http://www.nytimes.com/2010/12/31/us/politics/31holder.html.

24. Ibid.

25. Fund and von Spakovsky, *Obama's Enforcer*, 206.

26. Hans A. von Spakovsky, "Holder Winks at Voter Intimidation," *Heritage Foundation* (website), http://www.heritage.org/research/commentary/2009/06/holder-winks-at-voter-intimidation.

27. Markon and Thompson, "Dispute over New Black Panthers Case."

28. Ibid.

29. Ibid.

30. Department of Justice, Office of Professional Responsibility, Investigation of Dismissal of Defendants in *United States v. New Black Panther Party for Self-Defense*, March 17, 2001, at 62–64, http://democrats.judiciary.house.gov/sites/democrats.judiciary.house.gov/files/OPR%20Report_0.pdf.

31. Josh Gerstein, "Eric Holder: Black Panther Case Focus Demeans 'My

People,'" *Politico*, March 1, 2011, http://www.politico.com/blogs/joshgerstein/0311/Eric_Holder_Black_Panther_case_focus_demeans_my_people.html; Ed Hornick, "Holder 'Nation of Cowards' Remarks Blasted, Praised," CNN, February 19, 2009, http://www.cnn.com/2009/POLITICS/02/19/holder.folo.

32. Charlotte Allen, "Politicizing Justice," *Weekly Standard*, February 25, 2013, http://www.weeklystandard.com/articles/politicizing-justice_701329.html.

33. J. Christian Adams, *Injustice: Exposing the Racial Agenda of the Obama Justice Department* (Washington, DC: Regnery, 2011), 78.

34. Charlie Savage, "In Shift, Justice Department Is Hiring Lawyers with Civil Rights Backgrounds," *New York Times*, May 31, 2011, http://www.nytimes.com/2011/06/01/us/politics/01rights.html.

35. Ibid.

36. Brief for NAACP Legal Defense & Educational Fund, Inc. as Amicus Curiae Supporting Respondents, Parents Involved in Community Schools v. Seattle School Dist. No. 1, 551 U.S. 701 (2007) (No. 11-1507), 9, http://www.scotusblog.com/movabletype/archives/LDF.pdf.

37. OIG Report, "Review of the Operations of the Voting Section, 194–95.

38. Ibid., 82.

39. Fund and von Spakovsky, *Obama's Enforcer*, 29.

40. Ibid., 37.

41. US Department of Justice, Statement of the Attorney General on Litigation Involving the Defense of Marriage Act, February 23, 2011, http://www.justice.gov/opa/pr/statement-attorney-general-litigation-involving-defense-marriage-act.

42. Peter M. Shane, *Madison's Nightmare: How Executive Power Threatens American Democracy* (Chicago: University of Chicago Press, 2009), 127.

43. Ed Whelan, "DOMA Ruling Did Not 'Vindicate' Eric Holder," Bench Memos, *National Review*, September 29, 2014, http://www.nationalreview.com/bench-memos/389061/doma-ruling-did-not-vindicate-eric-holder-ed-whelan.

Chapter 3: A Leave of Absence from the "Republic of Conscience"

1. See Jack Goldsmith, "War Power," *Slate*, March 21, 2011, http://www.slate.com/articles/news_and_politics/jurisprudence/2011/03/war_power.html.

2. Harold Koh, *The National Security Constitution* (New Haven: Yale University Press, 1990), 130–31.

3. John M. Donnelly, "Pentagon Seeks Authority to Shift Millions to Cover Libya Expenses," *CQ Today Online News*, July 14, 2011, http://public .cq.com/docs/news/news-000003908296.html.

4. Daryl Levinson and Richard Pildes, "Separation of Parties, Not Powers," *Harvard Law Review* 119 (2006): 2311–2386.

5. General Accounting Office, Department of Defense—Compliance with Statutory Notification Requirement B-326013: Aug 21, 2014, http:// www.gao.gov/products/B-326013#mt=e-report.

6. Charlie Savage, "Barack Obama's Q&A," *Boston Globe*, December 20, 2007, http://www.boston.com/news/politics/2008/specials/Candidate QA/ObamaQA.

7. Daniel Klaidman, *Kill or Capture: The War on Terror and the Soul of the Obama Presidency* (New York: Houghton Mifflin Harcourt, 2012), 133.

8. Jon Hilsenrath, "Gates Says Libya Not Vital National Interest," *Wall Street Journal*, March 27, 2011, http://online.wsj.com/news/articles/SB1 0001424052748704308904576226704261420430?.

9. Office of Legal Counsel, Authority to Use Force in Libya, Memorandum Opinion for the Attorney General, April 1, 2011, 6, http://www .justice.gov/sites/default/files/olc/opinions/2011/04/31/authority -military-use-in-libya.pdf.

10. Ibid.

11. Ibid., 8.

12. For earlier examples, see Goldsmith, "War Power."

13. Koh, *National Security Constitution*, 39.

14. Charlie Savage, "2 Top Lawyers Lost to Obama in Libya War Policy Debate," *New York Times*, June 17, 2011, http://www.nytimes .com/2011/06/18/world/africa/18powers.html.

15. Jack Balkin, "George W. Obama and the OLC," *Balkinization* (blog), June 18, 2011, http://balkin.blogspot.com/2011/06/george-w-obama -and-olc.html.

16. See Nelson Lund, "Rational Choice at the Office of Legal Counsel," *Cardozo Law Review* 15 (1993): 437–506.

17. Harold Hongju Koh, Dean's Welcoming Speech, Yale Law School, August 30, 2006, http://www.law.yale.edu/documents/pdf/Deans_Office /Koh_welcome2006.pdf.

18. Klaidman, *Kill or Capture*, 141.

19. Quoted in Gene Healy, "Harold Koh Is the Gollum of Foggy Bottom: What Obama's Undeclared War in Libya Reveals about the Corrupting Effects of Power," *Reason.com*, June 21, 2011, http://reason.com/archives/2011/06/21/harold-koh-is-the-gollum-of-fo.

20. Koh, *National Security Constitution*, 69, 77.

21. Harold Hongju Koh and Aaron Zelinsky, "Practicing International Law in the Obama Administration," *Yale Journal of International Law Online* 35 (2009): 4, 9–10.

22. Klaidman, *Kill or Capture*, 140.

23. Ibid., 194.

24. Ibid., 214.

25. Ibid., 204.

26. E.g., Jeffrey Rosen, "Drone Strike Out: The Obama Administration's Drone Strike Memo Is Unconstitutional," *New Republic*, February 6, 2013, http://www.newrepublic.com/article/112338/obama-administrations-drone-memo-unconstitutional.

27. Department of Justice, Lawfulness of a Lethal Operation Directed against a U.S. Citizen Who Is a Senior Organizational Leader of Al-Qa'ida or an Associated Force, http://msnbcmedia.msn.com/i/msnbc/sections/news/020413_DOJ_White_Paper.pdf.

28. See Jack Goldsmith, "A Just Act of War," *New York Times*, September 30, 2011, http://www.nytimes.com/2011/10/01/opinion/a-just-act-of-war.html.

29. Ibid.

30. Klaidman, *Kill or Capture*, 219.

31. Ibid.

32. Jonathan Allen and John Bresnahan, "Sources: Joe Biden Likened Tea Partiers to Terrorists," *Politico*, August 1, 2011, http://www.politico.com/news/stories/0811/60421.html; Dave Boyer, "White House Compares GOP to Terrorists as Government Shutdown Nears," *Washington Times*, September 26, 2013, http://www.washingtontimes.com/news/2013/sep/26/white-house-compares-gop-terrorists-government-shu.

33. US Department of Justice, Attorney General Eric Holder Speaks at Northwestern University School of Law, March 5, 2012, http://www.justice.gov/iso/opa/ag/speeches/2012/ag-speech-1203051.html.

34. Glenn Greenwald, "Attorney General Holder Defends Execution without Charges," *Salon.com*, March 6, 2012, http://www.salon.com/2012/03/06/attorney_general_holder_defends_execution_without_charges.

35. Spencer S. Hsu, "Obama Invokes 'State Secrets' Claim to Dismiss Suit against Targeting of U.S. Citizen al-Aulaqi," *Washington Post*, September 25, 2010, http://www.washingtonpost.com/wp-dyn/content/article/2010/09/25/AR2010092500560_2.html?sid=ST2010092503098.

36. Mark Hosenball, "Secret Panel Can Put Americans on 'Kill List,'" Reuters, October 5, 2011, http://www.reuters.com/article/2011/10/05/us-cia-killlist-idUSTRE79475C20111005.

37. Quoted in Ed Brayton, "Irony and the Rule of Law, Part I," *FreeThought-Blogs.com*, December 6, 2011, http://freethoughtblogs.com/dispatches/2011/12/06/irony-and-the-rule-of-law-part-1.

38. White House Report on U.S. Actions in Libya, June 15, 2011, 25, http://www.nytimes.com/interactive/2011/06/16/us/politics/20110616_POWERS_DOC.html.

39. Ilya Somin, "The Growing Conflict over the Legality of the Libya Intervention," *Volokh Conspiracy* (blog), June 16, 2011, http://volokh.com/2011/06/16/the-growing-conflict-over-the-legality-of-the-libya-intervention.

40. Gene Healy, "White House: 'We Have Never Been at War in Northafrica!,'" *Cato at Liberty*, Cato Institute, June 16, 2011, http://www.cato.org/blog/white-house-we-have-never-been-war-northafrica.

41. Peter Spiro, "Latest on War Powers and Libya: Resurrecting the WPR? (Probably Not)," *Opinio Juris* (blog), June 16, 2011, http://opiniojuris.org/2011/06/16/latest-on-war-powers-and-libya-resurrecting-the-wpr-probably-not.

42. Jack Goldsmith, "Problems with the Obama Administration's War Powers Resolution Theory," *Lawfare* (blog), June 16, 2011, http://www.lawfareblog.com/2011/06/problems-with-the-obama-administration's-war-powers-resolution-theory-2/.

43. Ibid.

44. Koh, *National Security Constitution*, 131.

45. Akhil Reed Amar, "Bomb Away Mr. President," *Slate*, June 29, 2011, http://www.slate.com/articles/news_and_politics/jurisprudence/2011/06/bomb_away_mr_president.html.

46. "Harold Koh, Top Obama Lawyer, Defends Libya Operation over Congress' War Powers Objections," Reuters, June 28, 2011, http://www.huffingtonpost.com/2011/06/28/harold-koh-libya-obama-congress_n_886077.html.

47. Andrew Mangino, "At Yale, Koh Is a Liberal Lion," *Yale Daily News*, April

4, 2007, http://yaledailynews.com/blog/2007/04/04/at-law-school-koh -is-liberal-lion.

48. Quoted in Healy, "Harold Koh Is the Gollum."

49. Quoted in Charlie Savage, "Top State Dept. Lawyer Is Leaving," *New York Times*, December 12, 2012, http://thecaucus.blogs.nytimes .com/2012/12/12/top-state-dept-lawyer-is-leaving.

50. Eugene Volokh, "Former Yale Dean Harold Koh (Now Legal Adviser at the State Department) on Dealing with 'Hate Speech' by 'Applying . . . the Transnationalist Approach to Judicial Interpretation,'" *Volokh Conspiracy* (blog), September 13, 2012, http://volokh.com/2012/09/13 /former-yale-dean-harold-koh-now-attorney-advisor-at-the-state-de partment-on.

51. Harold Hongju Koh, "On American Exceptionalism," *Stanford Law Review* 55 (2003): 1479–1527.

52. U.N. Security Council Resolution 1973 (2011).

53. Richard Leiby and Muhammad Mansour, "Arab League Asks U.N. for No-fly Zone over Libya," *Washington Post*, March 22, 2011, http://www .washingtonpost.com/world/arab-league-asks-un-for-no-fly-zone-over -libya/2011/03/12/ABoieoR_story.html.

54. Ryan Lizza, "The Consequentialist: How the Arab Spring Remade Obama's Foreign Policy," *New Yorker*, May 2, 2011, http://www.new yorker.com/magazine/2011/05/02/the-consequentialist.

55. Koh, "On American Exceptionalism."

56. See Ken I. Kersch, *Constructing Civil Liberties: Discontinuities in the Development of American Constitutional Law* (Cambridge, UK: Cambridge University Press, 2004), 338–61.

Chapter 4: The Assault on Private Property and Freedom of Contract

1. Todd Zywicki, "The Auto Bailout and the Rule of Law," *National Affairs*, Spring 2011, http://www.nationalaffairs.com/publications/detail/the -auto-bailout-and-the-rule-of-law.

2. Quoted in Gene Healy, *The Cult of the Presidency* (Washington, DC: Cato Institute, 2009), 304.

3. Zywicki, "The Auto Bailout."

4. David E. Sanger, "The 31-Year-Old in Charge of Dismantling G.M.," *New York Times*, May 31, 2009, http://www.nytimes.com/2009/06/01 /business/01deese.html.

5. Steven Rattner, *Overhaul: An Insider's Account of the Obama Administration's Emergency Rescue of the Auto Industry* (New York: Houghton Mifflin Harcourt, 2010), 210.
6. Ibid.,187.
7. Zywicki, "The Auto Bailout."
8. Ibid.
9. Ibid.
10. Ibid.
11. Ibid.
12. Ibid.
13. David Freddoso, *Gangster Government* (Washington, DC: Regnery 2011), 34.
14. Quoted in Freddoso, *Gangster Government*, 44.
15. Barack Obama, "On Chrysler and the Autos," video, 12:22, April 30, 2009, http://www.whitehouse.gov/video/On-Chrysler-and-the-Autos.
16. *In re* ChryslerLLC, 576 F.3d 108, 120 (2d Cir. 2009).
17. Indiana Police Pension Trust v. Chrysler LLC, 558 U.S. 1087 (2009); see Ilya Shapiro and Cory L. Andrews, "High Court Erases Precedent in Chrysler Bankruptcy," Washington Legal Foundation, January 15, 2010, http://object.cato.org/sites/cato.org/files/articles/shapiro-WLF -Chrysler-Bankruptcy.pdf.
18. Zywicki, "The Auto Bailout."
19. James Sherk and Todd Zywicki, "Auto Bailout or UAW Bailout? Taxpayer Losses Came from Subsidizing Union Compensation," Backgrounder No. 2700, Heritage Foundation, June 23, 2012, http://www.heritage .org/research/reports/2012/06/auto-bailout-or-uaw-bailout-taxpayer -losses-came-from-subsidizing-union-compensation.
20. Gene Healy, "Obama's Executive Unilateralism," Cato Institute, June 19, 2012, http://www.cato.org/publications/commentary/obamas-ex ecutive-unilateralism.
21. Susan Crabtree, "Health and Human Services Quietly Giving Unions Obamacare Fix," *Washington Examiner*, November 6, 2013, http:// washingtonexaminer.com/health-and-human-services-quietly-giving -unions-obamacare-fix/article/2538621.
22. Complaint, Boeing v. International Assoc. of Machinists, Case 19-CA-32431, http://www.nlrb.gov/sites/default/files/attachments/basic -page/node-3310/cpt_19-ca-032431_boeing__4-20-2011_complaint_and _not_hrg.pdf.

23. Answer, Boeing v. International Assoc. of Machinists, Case 19-CA-32431, http://www.nlrb.gov/sites/default/files/attachments/basic-page/node-3310/boeing_answer_final_19-ca-032431_2.pdf.
24. Steven Greenhouse, "Labor Board Drops Case against Boeing after Union Reaches Accord," *New York Times*, December 29, 2011, http://www.nytimes.com/2011/12/10/business/labor-board-drops-case-against-boeing.html.
25. Richard Posner, "Abuse of Presidential Power," *Becker-Posner Blog*, July 18, 2010, http://www.becker-posner-blog.com/2010/07/abuse-of-presidential-power-posner.html.
26. Ricardo Alonso-Zaldivar, "Insurance Industry Agrees to Fix Kids Coverage Gap," AP, March 30, 2010, http://www.huffingtonpost.com/huff-wires/20100329/us-health-overhaul-children-s-coverage.
27. Ibid.
28. Ibid.
29. Posner, "Abuse of Presidential Power."
30. Sackett v. EPA, 622 F.3d 1139 (9th Cir. 2010).
31. Sackett v. EPA, 132 S. Ct. 1367 (2012).
32. Ibid. at 1375 (Alito, J., concurring).
33. Ark. Game & Fish Comm'n, 133 S. Ct. 511 (2012).
34. Ark. Game & Fish Comm'n v. United States, 637 F.3d 1366 (Fed. Cir. 2011).
35. Ark. Game & Fish Comm'n, 133 S. Ct. at 515.
36. Horne v. Dep't of Agric., 133 S. Ct. 2053, 2061 (2013).
37. Zach Weissmueller, "*USDA v. Horne*: Farmers Fight to Keep Their Own Raisins," *Reason.com*, July 18, 2013, http://reason.com/reasontv/2013/07/18/usda-v-horne-farmers-fight-for-their-rig.
38. Ibid.
39. *Horne*, 133 S. Ct. at 2059, n. 3.
40. Quoted in Weissmuller, "*USDA v. Horne*."
41. Ibid.
42. Horne v. U.S. Dep't of Agric., 673 F.3d 1071, 1078 (9th Cir. 2011).
43. *Horne*, 133 S. Ct. at 2063.
44. Horne v. Dept. of Agriculture, 576 U.S. __ (2015).

Chapter 5: "More Czars Than the Romanovs"

1. Onan Coca, "Viral Video of Obama in 2008 Implying Executive Orders Are Unconstitutional," *Eagle Rising* (website), February 15, 2014,

http://eaglerising.com/4692/viral-video-obama-2008-implying-execu
tive-orders-unconstitutional.

2. John McCain, @SenJohnMcCain, Twitter, May 30, 2009, https://twit
ter.com/SenJohnMcCain/status/1972425520.

3. Mitchel A. Sollenberger and Mark J. Rozell, *The President's Czars: Undermining Congress and the Constitution* (Lawrence: University of Kansas
Press, 2012), 7.

4. Ibid., 76–77, 163.

5. Ibid., 161.

6. Ibid., 140.

7. Sharyl Attkisson, "EPA in Contempt for Destroying Computer Files,"
SharylAttkisson.com, June 21, 2014, http://sharylattkisson.com/epa-in
-contempt-for-destroying-computer-files.

8. Sollenberger and Rozell, *The President's Czars*, 152.

9. Michael Burnham, "Embattled Van Jones Quits, but 'Czar' Debates
Rage On," *Greenwire* (website), September 9, 2009, http://www.ny
times.com/gwire/2009/09/08/08greenwire-embattled-van-jones
-quits-but-czar-debates-rage-9373.html.

10. Van Jones, individual profile, *Discoverthenetworks.org*, http://www
.discoverthenetworks.org/individualProfile.asp?indid=2406.

11. Sollenberger and Rozell, *The President's Czars*, 154.

12. Ibid., 158.

13. Ibid., 158–59.

14. Ibid., 159.

15. Ibid., 149.

16. Ibid., 150.

17. Steven Rattner, *Overhaul: An Insider's Account of the Obama Administration's Emergency Rescue of the Auto Industry* (New York: Houghton Mifflin
Harcourt, 2010), 151.

18. "Obama's Czar Ron Bloom Agrees with Mao—Address at Investor Conf
part 3," YouTube video, 1:19, posted by "Don't Mess with America!," September 12, 2009, https://www.youtube.com/watch?v=RCvQ8BSUv-g.

19. Sollenberger and Rozell, *The President's Czars*, 155.

20. Noelle Straub, "Sen. Byrd Questions Obama's Use of Policy 'Czars,'"
Greenwire (website), February 25, 2009, http://www.nytimes.com
/gwire/2009/02/25/25greenwire-byrd-questions-obamas-use-of-policy
-czars-9865.html.

21. Sollenberger and Rozell, *The President's Czars*, 155.

22. Aaron J. Saiger, "Obama's 'Czars' for Domestic Policy and the Law of the White House Staff," *Fordham Law Review* 79 (2011): 2577, 2604.

23. Margaret Kriz Hobson, "Issa's Oversight Agenda to Challenge Obama," *CQ Today*, November 3, 2010; Brian Friel, "Where Will the G.O.P. Go Digging?," *New York Times*, November 14, 2010, http://www.nytimes.com/2010/11/14/opinion/14friel.html.

24. Bruce Ackerman, "Obama, Warren and the Imperial Presidency," *Wall Street Journal*, September 22, 2010, http://online.wsj.com/news/articles/SB10001424052748703989304575503661726493580.

25. Brady Dennis and Scott Wilson, "Obama Ignores Critics, Appoints Warren to Set Up Consumer Protection Agency," *Washington Post*, September 17, 2010, http://www.washingtonpost.com/wp-dyn/content/article/2010/09/17/AR2010091706597.html.

26. Sewell Chan, "Interim Plan for Warren Raises Even Supporters' Eyebrows," *New York Times*, September 16, 2010, http://www.nytimes.com/2010/09/17/business/17warren.html.

27. Ibid.

28. Department of Defense and Full-Year Continuing Appropriations Act, H.R. 1473, 112th Cong. § 2262 (2011).

29. "Do You Promise Not to Use Signing Statements? Candidate Obama in '08 'Yes'," YouTube video, 3:25, from a campaign event in Billings, Montana, on May 19, 2008, posted by CNS News, April 11, 2011, https://www.youtube.com/watch?v=4iGAgocmI54&feature.

30. Charlie Savage, *Takeover: The Return of the Imperial Presidency and the Subversion of American Democracy* (New York: Little Brown, 2007), 232.

31. Peter Shane, *Madison's Nightmare: How Executive Power Threatens American Democracy* (Chicago: University of Chicago, 2009), 130.

32. Savage, *Takeover*, 235.

33. Ibid.

34. Ibid., 230.

35. Ibid., 243.

36. Ibid.

37. Report, ABA Task Force on Presidential Signing Statements and the Separation of Powers Doctrine (July 24, 2006), American Bar Association, http://www.coherentbabble.com/signingstatements/ABATaskForceReport.pdf.

38. Shane, *Madison's Nightmare*, 133.

39. Quoted in Sollenberger and Rozell, *The President's Czars*, 155.

40. Ibid., 171.
41. Ibid.
42. Ibid.
43. Saiger, "Obama's 'Czars' for Domestic Policy," 2604.
44. Sollenberger and Rozell, *The President's Czars,* 155.
45. John Elwood, "Now THAT Is a Signing Statement!," *Volokh Conspiracy* (blog), January 3, 2013, http://www.volokh.com/2013/01/03/now-that-is-a-signing-statement.
46. Saiger, "Obama's 'Czars' for Domestic Policy," 2589.
47. Anne E. Kornblut, "White House Moving to Repair Troubled Relationship with Cabinet," *Washington Post,* March 9, 2011, http://www.washingtonpost.com/wp-dyn/content/article/2011/03/08/AR2011030805751.html.
48. J. R. Dunn, "Cracking the Czars," *American Thinker,* August 7, 2013, http://www.americanthinker.com/2013/08/cracking_the_czars.html.

Chapter 6: Obamacare above All

1. See Josh Blackman, *Unprecedented: The Constitutional Challenge to Obamacare* (New York: PublicAffairs, 2013), 283.
2. E.g., Jacqueline Klingebiel, "Obama: Mandate Is Not a Tax," *ABCNews.com,* September 20, 2009, http://abcnews.go.com/blogs/politics/2009/09/obama-mandate-is-not-a-tax.
3. "Obama Administration Knew Millions Could Not Keep Their Health Insurance," NBC News, October 28, 2013, http://www.nbcnews.com/news/other/obama-admin-knew-millions-could-not-keep-their-health-insurance-f8C11484394.
4. Jordan Fabian, "Key Senate Democrat Suggests That He Didn't Read Entire Healthcare Reform Bill," *The Hill,* August 25, 2010, http://thehill.com/blogs/blog-briefing-room/news/115749-sen-baucus-suggests-he-did-not-read-entire-health-bill.
5. Wickard v. Filburn, 317 U.S. 111 (1942).
6. See David Bernstein, "Equal Protection for Economic Liberty: Is the Court Ready?," Cato Institute, October 1992, http://www.cato.org/pubs/pas/pa-181es.html.
7. United States v. Morrison, 529 U.S. 598 (2000); United States v. Lopez, 514 U.S. 549 (1995).
8. E.g., Larry D. Kramer, *The People Themselves: Popular Constitutionalism and Judicial Review* (New York: Oxford University Press, 2004).

9. Gonzales v. Raich, 545 U.S. 1 (2005).
10. David Bernstein, "Democratic Congressman and Senators on Constitutional Authority for the ACA," *Volokh Conspiracy* (blog), March 28, 2012, http://volokh.com/2012/03/28/democratic-congressman-and-senators-on-constitutional-authority-for-the-aca/.
11. For a comprehensive and well-written overview of how the Obamacare litigation unfolded, see Blackman, *Unprecedented*. For a recap of how the anti-Obamacare constitutional arguments developed on the influential Volokh Conspiracy blog, see Trevor Burrus, ed., *A Conspiracy against Obamacare: The Volokh Conspiracy and the Healthcare Case* (New York: Palgrave Macmillan, 2013).
12. David Bernstein, "Origins of Commerce Clause Objections to the Individual Mandate," *Volokh Conspiracy* (blog), June 11, 2012, http://volokh.com/2012/06/11/origins-of-commerce-clause-objections-to-the-individual-mandate/.
13. Ron Suskind, *Confidence Men* (New York: Harper Perennial, 2011).
14. Josh Blackman, "Obamacare & Man at Yale," *University of Illinois Law Review* 2014 (2014): 1241, 1245.
15. David Bernstein, "Has the Pro-ACA Side Come Up with a 'Limiting Principle'?," *Volokh Conspiracy* (blog), March 27, 2012, http://volokh.com/2012/03/27/has-the-pro-aca-side-come-up-with-a-limiting-principle.
16. David Bernstein, "A Bug or a Feature?," *Volokh Conspiracy* (blog), March 20, 2012, http://volokh.com/2012/03/20/a-bug-or-a-feature.
17. Jan Crawford, "Roberts Switched Views to Uphold Health Care Law," CBS News, July 1, 2012, http://www.cbsnews.com/8301-3460_162-57464549/roberts-switchedviews-touphold-health-care-law.
18. See Randy E. Barnett, "The Disdain Campaign," *Harvard Law Review Forum* 126:1 (2012).
19. See, e.g., Carrie Budoff Brown and Jennifer Epstein, "Obama, the Left Take on Supreme Court," April 3, 2012, *Politico*, http://www.politico.com/news/stories/0412/74759.html.
20. National Federation of Independent Business v. Sebelius, 132 S. Ct. 2566 (2012).
21. Ibid.
22. Quin Hillyer, "Obamacare's Hideous History, Recounted," *American Spectator*, July 3, 2012, http://spectator.org/articles/35226/obamacares-hideous-history-recounted.
23. Ibid.

24. Ibid.
25. See Diane Cohen and Michael F. Cannon, "The Independent Payment Advisory Board: PPACA's Anti-Constitutional and Authoritarian Super-Legislature," *Cato Policy Analysis* no. 700, June 14, 2012, http://www.cato.org/publications/policy-analysis/independent-payment-advisory-board-ppacas-anticonstitutional-authoritarian-superlegislature.
26. This has been an Obama Administration *modus operandi* in a variety of contexts. See Josh Blackman, "The Constitutionality of DAPA Part II: Faithfully Executing the Law," *Texas Review of Law & Politics* 19 (2015): 213–85; Juliet Eilperin, "White House Delayed Enacting Rules Ahead of 2012 Election to Avoid Controversy," *Washington Post*, December 14, 2013, http://www.washingtonpost.com/politics/white-house-delayed-enacting-rules-ahead-of-2012-election-to-avoid-controversy/2013/12/14/7885a494-561a-11e3-ba82-16ed03681809_story.html.
27. Mark J. Mazur, "Continuing to Implement the ACA in a Careful, Thoughtful Manner," Treasury Notes, July 2, 2013, http://www.treasury.gov/connect/blog/Pages/Continuing-to-Implement-the-ACA-in-a-Careful-Thoughtful-Manner-.aspx.
28. Shared Responsibility for Employers Regarding Health Coverage, 79 Fed. Reg. 8544, 8574 (2014).
29. Letter from Gary Cohen, Director, Center for Consumer Information & Insurance Oversight, Department of Health & Human Services, to State Insurance Commissioners (November 14, 2013).
30. Ezra Klein, "The Individual Mandate No Longer Applies to People Whose Plans Were Canceled," *Washington Post*, December 19, 2013, http://www.washingtonpost.com/blogs/wonkblog/wp/2013/12/19/the-obama-administration-just-delayed-the-individual-mandate-for-people-whose-plans-have-been-canceled.
31. Josh Blackman, "Obamacare and Government by Blog Post," *Online Library of Law and Liberty* (website), March 10, 2014, http://www.libertylawsite.org/2014/03/10/obamacare-and-government-by-blog-post.
32. Justin Sink, "White House Threatens Veto of Upton Bill," *The Hill*, November 14, 2013, http://thehill.com/homenews/administration/190365-white-house-threatens-veto-of-upton-bill.
33. Nicholas Bagley, "The Legality of Delaying Key Elements of the ACA," *New England Journal of Medicine* (May 22, 2014): 1967–69.
34. Ibid., 1969.
35. Ibid.

36. Zachary Price, "Enforcement Discretion and Executive Duty," *Vanderbilt Law Review* 67 (2014): 675.

37. "#GruberGate," *Powerline* (blog), July 31, 2014, http://www.powerline blog.com/archives/2014/07/grubergate.php.

38. Oversight Committee Asks IRS to Explain Recent Rule That Expands Obamacare's Reach in a Way Not Authorized in Law, House Oversight Committee, August 22, 2012, http://oversight.house.gov/release/over sight-committee-asks-irs-to-explain-recent-rule-that-expands-obama cares-reach-in-a-way-not-authorized-in-law; David Weigel, "House Republicans Want to Resuscitate Obamacare-Killing Lawsuit," *Bloomberg News*, September 29, 2014, http://www.bloomberg.com/politics/ar ticles/2014-09-29/house-republicans-want-to-resuscitate-an-obamacare -killing-lawsuit.

39. Michael S. Greve, "Halbig and Obamacare: What We Have Learned (Part II)," *Online Library of Law and Liberty* (website), August 6, 2014, http://www.libertylawsite.org/2014/08/06/halbig-and-obamacare- what-we-have-learned-part-ii.

40. King v. Burwell, 576 U.S. ___ (2015).

41. Ibid.

42. E.g., Sarah Kliff, "Budget Request Denied, Sebelius Turns to Health Executives to Finance Obamacare," *Washington Post*, May 10, 2013, http://www.washingtonpost.com/blogs/wonkblog/wp/2013/05/10 /budget-request-denied-sebelius-turns-to-health-executives-to-finance -obamacare; "Did the Obama Administration Pressure Insurance Companies?," CNN, October 29, 2013, http://www.cnn.com/videos/best oftv/2013/10/29/ac-wh-pressures-insurers.cnn; Michael F. Cannon, "ObamaCare's Threat to Free Speech," *Cato at Liberty*, Cato Institute, September 13, 2010, http://www.cato.org/blog/obamacares-threat -free-speech.

43. Michael F. Cannon, "Bland CBO Memo, or Smoking Gun?," *Cato at Liberty*, Cato Institute, December 16, 2009, http://www.cato.org/blog /bland-cbo-memo-or-smoking-gun.

44. Editorial, "The Obama Hiatus," *Wall Street Journal*, June 15, 2011, http:// www.wsj.com/articles/SB10001424052702303848104576385620186823528.

45. Michael F. Cannon, "Congress's Obamacare Waiver," *National Review*, August 8, 2013, http://www.nationalreview.com/article/355176/con gresss-obamacare-waiver-michael-f-cannon.

46. "What's Obama's Health Reform Costing? More Than $73 Billion to

Date: BGOV Analysis," Bloomberg Government, September 24, 2014, http://about.bgov.com/bgov200/content/uploads/sites/2/2014/09/ACA-ppt-FINAL_Rev.pdf.

47. Tyler Hartsfield and Grace-Marie Turner, "47 Changes to Obamacare . . . So Far," Galen Institute, January 7, 2015, http://www.galen.org/newsletters/changes-to-obamacare-so-far.

Chapter 7: You Can't Say That!

1. Citizens United v. FEC, 130 S. Ct. 876 (2011).
2. See, e.g., Lachlan Markay, "Democracy Alliance President: Campaign Finance Reform a Means to Push Liberal Policy Goals," *Washington Free Beacon*, July 10, 2014, http://freebeacon.com/politics/democracy-alliancepresident-campaign-finance-reform-a-means-to-push-liberal-policy-goals.
3. Brian Mooney, "In a Shift, Obama Rejects Public Funding," *Boston Globe*, June 20, 2008, http://www.boston.com/news/nation/articles/2008/06/20/in_a_shift_obama_rejects_public_funding; Jonathan D. Salant, "Spending Doubled as Obama Led Billion-Dollar Campaign," *Bloomberg News*, December 27, 2008, http://www.bloomberg.com/apps/news?sid=anLDS9WWPQW8&pid=newsarchive.
4. Transcript of Oral Argument, Citizens United v. FEC, March 24, 2009, http://demo.tizra.com/08-205-Citizens-United-v-Federal-Election-Commission-Oral-Argument-Transcript/40.
5. Ibid.
6. She didn't mention that the FEC had, however, tried to restrict magazines in the past, and had also spent four years investigating a brochure advertising a book by George Soros. FEC v. Phillips Publishing, Inc., 517 F. Supp. 1308 (1981); see Reader's Digest Association, Inc. v. FEC, 509 F. Supp. 1210 (S.D.N.Y. 1981) (dissemination of videotapes critical of Senator Ted Kennedy); MUR 5642 (2009) (George Soros), http://eqs.fec.gov/eqsdocsMUR/29044223840.pdf.
7. Transcript of Oral Argument, Citizens United v. FEC, September 9, 2009, http://www.supremecourt.gov/oral_arguments/argument_transcripts/08-205%5BReargued%5D.pdf.
8. White House Office of the Press Secretary, Statement from the President on Today's Supreme Court Decision, January 21, 2010, http://www.whitehouse.gov/the-press-office/statement-president-todays-supreme-court-decision-0.

9. James Marc Leas and Rob Hager, "The Problem with Citizens United Is Not Corporate Personhood," *Truthout,* January 17, 2012, http://www.truth-out.org/news/item/6095:the-problem-with-citizens-united-is-not-corporate-personhood.

10. Robert Barnes, "Reactions Split on Obama's Remark, Alito's Response at State of the Union," *Washington Post,* January 29, 2010, http://www.washingtonpost.com/wp-dyn/content/article/2010/01/28/AR2010012802893.html.

11. Any doubts about the scope of *Citizens United* with regard to foreign political contributions were laid to rest in 2012, when the Supreme Court unanimously upheld a federal law banning foreign entities from spending money on American political campaigns. Bluman v. FEC, 132 S. Ct. 1087 (2012). That didn't stop the president from reiterating in January 2015 the lie that *Citizens United* allowed foreign corporations to "spend unlimited amounts of money to influence our elections." Rick Hasen, "President Obama Issues False Statement on Citizens United," *Election Law Blog,* January 21, 2015, http://electionlawblog.org/?p=69806.

12. Barnes, "Reactions Split on Obama's Remark."

13. John D. McKinnon and Martin Vaughan, "Democrats Criticize Group over Attack Ads, Tax Violations," *Wall Street Journal,* August 26, 2010, http://online.wsj.com/articles/SB10001424052748704147804575456083141366918.

14. "This Week" Transcript: Axelrod, McConnell, and Queen Rania, ABCNews.go.com, September 26, 2010, http://abcnews.go.com/ThisWeek/week-transcript-axelrod-mcconnell-queen-rania/story?id=11729101&page=5.

15. David Bernstein, "Brouhaha over the Koch Brothers," *Volokh Conspiracy* (blog), August 30, 2010, http://www.volokh.com/2010/08/30/brouhaha-over-the-koch-brothers/.

16. Jane Mayer, "Covert Operations," *New Yorker,* August 30, 2010, http://www.newyorker.com/magazine/2010/08/30/covert-operations.

17. Ibid.

18. Faiz Shakir, "TP's Lee Fang Discusses the 'Kochtopus' Network on Countdown," *ThinkProgress* (website), August 25, 2010, http://thinkprogress.org/politics/2010/08/25/115558/lee-on-kochs/.

19. Open Society Institute, Job Posting for Communications Officer, DevNet Jobs, http://216.197.119.113/cgi-bin/jobman/exec/view.cgi?archive=169&num=68537.

20. Lori Montgomery, "GOP Senators Seek Probe over U.S. Remarks on Koch Industries," *Washington Post*, September 24, 2010, http://www.washingtonpost.com/wp-dyn/content/article/2010/09/24/AR 2010092405229.html.

21. Ibid.

22. John McCormack, "Goolsbee's Mysterious Tweet about the Koch Brothers' Taxes," *Weekly Standard*, May 29, 2013, http://www.weekly standard.com/blogs/former-white-house-official-deletes-embarrass ing-tweet-about-koch-brothers-taxes_731862.html.

23. Eilana Johnson, "The Missing Koch Report," *National Review Online*, August 20, 2013, http://www.nationalreview.com/article/356260/miss ing-koch-report-eliana-johnson.

24. "Big Oil Billionaire Koch Brothers Funding Swift-Boat Attacks on House Democrats," Democratic Congressional Campaign Committee, September 2, 2010, http://archive.dccc.org/blog/entry/big_oil_billion aire_koch_brothers_funding_swift-boat_attacks_on_house_.

25. Lynn Jenkins, "Working on Excuses," *Washington Times*, October 10, 2010, http://www.washingtontimes.com/news/2010/oct/6/working -on-excuses.

26. Sam Stein, "Obama, Dems Try to Make Shadowy Conservative Groups a Problem for Conservatives," *Huffington Post*, September 21, 2010, http://www.huffingtonpost.com/2010/09/21/obama-dems-try-to -make-sh_n_733133.html.

27. Burgess Everett, "Reid: Kochs 'Main Causes' of Climate Change," *Politico*, May 7, 2014, http://www.politico.com/story/2014/05/harry -reid-koch-brothers-climate-change-106441.html.

28. Andy Kroll, "How the Koch Brothers Backed Public-School Segregation," *Mother Jones*, August 15, 2011, http://www.motherjones.com /mojo/2011/08/koch-brothers-school-segregation-americans -prosperity.

29. John Hinderaker, "Washington Post Falls for Left-Wing Fraud, Embarrasses Itself," *Powerline* (blog), March 20, 2014, http://www .powerlineblog.com/archives/2014/03/washington-post-falls-for-left -wing-fraud-embarrasses-itself.php.

30. Erick Erickson, "MSNBC's Karen Finney Says the Koch Brothers Killed Trayvon Martin," *RedState* (website), March 23, 2012, http://www .redstate.com/diary/Erick/2012/03/23/msnbcs-karen-finney-says-the -koch-brothers-killed-trayvon-martin.

31. Ari Berman, "Why the Koch Brothers and ALEC Don't Want You to Vote," *The Nation*, November 8, 2011, http://www.thenation.com/blog/164453/why-koch-brothers-and-alec-dont-want-you-vote.

32. Quoted in "A Letter to the Obama Campaign," *KochFacts.com*, February 24, 2012, http://www.kochfacts.com/kf/obamaletter.

33. Lee Fang, "The Contango Game: How Koch Industries Manipulates the Oil Market for Profit," *ThinkProgress* (website), April 13, 2011, http://thinkprogress.org/economy/2011/04/13/153206/koch-industries-price-gouging.

34. Department of Justice Office of Public Affairs, "Attorney General Holder Announces Formation of Oil and Gas Price Fraud Working Group to Focus on Energy Markets," April 21, 2011, http://www.justice.gov/opa/pr/2011/April/11-ag-500.html.

35. http://www.kochaddiction.com/#meetkochs.

36. Aaron Blake, "Reid: Koch Brothers Are 'Un-American,'" *Washington Post*, February 27, 2014, http://www.washingtonpost.com/blogs/post-politics/wp/2014/02/27/reid-koch-brothers-are-un-american/.

37. Chris Cillizza, "Koch Zero? Why Democrats Are Going to Have a Hard Time Enraging People about Campaign Finance," *Washington Post*, March 25, 2014, http://www.washingtonpost.com/blogs/the-fix/wp/2014/03/25/why-attacking-the-koch-brothers-probably-wont-work.

38. "Pat Roberts Addresses Harry Reid's 'Koch Addiction,'" *Daily Caller* (website), May 21, 2014, http://dailycaller.com/2014/05/21/intervention-pat-roberts-addresses-harry-reids-koch-addiction-video/.

39. Mattea Gold, "Ted Cruz Accuses Harry Reid of 'Slander Campaign' against Koch Brothers," *Washington Post*, September 9, 2014, http://www.washingtonpost.com/blogs/post-politics/wp/2014/09/09/ted-cruz-accuses-harry-reid-of-slander-campaign-against-koch-brothers.

40. Theresa Agovino, "David Koch Offers Rare Look into His Giving, Politics," *Crain's New York Business*, September 8, 2014, http://www.crainsnewyork.com/article/20140908/NONPROFITS/309079993/david-koch-offers-rare-look-into-his-giving-politics.

41. Kim Strassel, "Those Koch Attacks Are Working," *Wall Street Journal*, August 21, 2014, http://online.wsj.com/articles/kim-strassel-those-koch-attacks-are-working-1408663354.

42. Jess Bravin and Brody Mullins, "New Rules Proposed on Campaign Donors," *Wall Street Journal*, February 12, 2010, http://www.wsj.com/articles/SB10001424052748703382904575059941933737002.

43. "ACLU Urges No Vote on DISCLOSE Act," *ACLU.org*, July 26, 2010, https://www.aclu.org/free-speech/aclu-urges-no-vote-disclose-act.

44. "Senators Call for IRS Investigations into Potential Abuse of Tax-Exempt Status by Groups Engaged in Campaign Activity," *Bennet.Senate.gov*, February 16, 2012, http://www.bennet.senate.gov/newsroom/press /release/senators-call-for-irs-investigations-into-potential-abuse-of-tax -exempt-status-by-groups-engaged-in-campaign-activity.

45. E.g., Representative Peter Welch et al., Letter to Commissioner Shulman, March 28, 2012, http://images.politico.com/global/2012/06 /welch_request.html.

46. See, e.g., "IRS at the Crossroads," *Wall Street Journal*, April 9, 2014, http://online.wsj.com/articles/SB100014240527023039104045794900414770592588.

47. Paul Caron, "House Releases Report on Lois Lerner's Role in the IRS Scandal," *Tax Prof Blog*, March 11, 2014, http://taxprof.typepad.com/tax prof_blog/2014/03/house-releases-.html.

48. "IRS Documents Reveal Agency Flagged Groups for 'Anti-Obama Rhetoric,' Big Three Refuse to Report," *Wall Street Journal*, September 24, 2014, http://online.wsj.com/news/articles/SB10001424052702304213904579093491966449908.

49. Treasury Inspector General for Tax Administration, Ref. No. 2013-10-053, Inappropriate Criteria Were Used to Identify Tax-Exempt Applications for Review (May 2013), http://www.treasury.gov/tigta/auditreports /2013reports/201310053fr.pdf.

50. "The IRS Harassment Scandal: A Timeline of 'Reform,'" Center for Competitive Politics, http://www.campaignfreedom.org/wp-content /uploads/2013/09/2013-09-16_Timeline_IRS-Scandal_Documenting -Efforts-By-The-Regulatory-Community-To-Police-Political-Speech -Full-Version-1.pdf.

51. Sharyl Attkisson and Kim Skeen, "What's Going On between the IRS and True the Vote," CBS News, May 29, 2013, http://www.cbsnews .com/news/whats-going-on-between-the-irs-and-true-the-vote; Steven Dinan, "House Republicans Find 10% of Tea Party Donors Audited by IRS," *Washington Times*, May 7, 2014, http://www.washingtontimes .com/news/2014/may/7/house-republicans-find-10-of-tea-party -donors-audi; Gayle Trotter, "Christine O'Donnell's IRS Case Reveals More Than Just a 'Smidgen of Corruption,'" *Daily Caller* (website), February 28, 2014, http://dailycaller.com/2014/02/28/christine-odonnells -irs-case-reveals-more-than-just-a-smidgen-of-corruption.

52. E.g., Hatch, "11 Others to IRS: Don't Let Politics Trump Policy on Non-Profit Group Designations," *Hatch.Senate.gov*, March 14, 2012, http://www.hatch.senate.gov/public/index.cfm/2012/3/hatch-11-others-to-irs-don-t-let-politics-trump-policy-on-non-profit-group-designations; Sarah Swinehart, "Camp Demands IRS Answer Questions about Gift Tax Investigation Exercises Authority to Review Non-Public Information," *HouseWaysandMeans.gov*, June 15, 2011, http://waysandmeans.house.gov/news/documentsingle.aspx?DocumentID=246630.

53. Sue Reisinger, "IRS Chief Counsel Continues to Draw Critical Fire," *Corporate Counsel* (website), July 29, 2013, http://www.corpcounsel.com/id=1202612653261/IRS-Chief-Counsel-Continues-to-Draw-Critical-Fire.

54. White House Office of the Press Secretary, Statement by the President, May 15, 2013, http://www.whitehouse.gov/the-press-office/2013/05/15/statement-president.

55. Josh Hicks, "Obama Political Donor Leading Justice Department's IRS Investigation," *Washington Post*, January 9, 2014, http://www.washingtonpost.com/blogs/federal-eye/wp/2014/01/09/obama-political-donor-leading-justice-departments-irs-investigation.

56. Stephen Dinan, "Feds Pick Obama Supporter to Lead Probe into IRS Tea Party Targeting," *Washington Times*, January 8, 2014, http://www.washingtontimes.com/news/2014/jan/8/feds-pick-obama-supporter-lead-irs-tea-party-probe.

57. Lois G. Lerner, Email of February 1, 2011, http://oversight.house.gov/wp-content/uploads/2014/03/2157-Color-Copier@mail.house_.gov_20140304_215233.pdf.

58. "'Not Even a Smidgen of Corruption': Obama Downplays IRS, Other Scandals," *FoxNews.com*, February 3, 2014, http://www.foxnews.com/politics/2014/02/03/not-even-smidgen-corruption-obama-downplays-irs-other-scandals.

59. National Taxpayer Advocate Special Report to Congress: Political Activity and the Rights of Applicants for Tax-Exempt Status, June 30, 2013, http://www.taxpayeradvocate.irs.gov/2014ObjectivesReport/Special-Report.

60. Nan Aron, "Treasury, IRS Proposal: The End of Nonpartisan Election Work by 501(c)(4)s?," *Bolder Advocacy* (website), November 27, 2013, http://bolderadvocacy.org/blog/treasury-and-irs-proposal-endangers-citizen-participation-in-democracy.

61. Laura W. Murphy, " 'Fixing' *Citizens United* Will Break the Constitution," *ACLU.org*, June 28, 2012, https://www.aclu.org/blog/free-speech/fix ing-citizens-united-will-break-constitution.

62. Daniel Salzman, "Senator Ted Cruz Believes *Citizens United* Amend ment Would Criminalize *Saturday Night Live*," *Flicksided* (website), http://flicksided.com/2014/09/10/senator-ted-cruz-believes-citizens -united-amendment-criminalize-saturday-night-live.

Chapter 8: Antidiscrimination Law Run Amok

1. Compare Dayton Christian Schools, Inc. v. Ohio Civil Rights Commis sion, 766 F.2d 932 (6th Cir.), vacated on ripeness grounds, 477 U.S. 619 (1986), with McLeod v. Providence Christian School, 408 N.W.2d 146, 152 (Mich. 1987).

2. E.g., Lewis ex. rel. Murphy v. Buchanan, 1979 WL 29147 (D. Minn.).

3. Ganzy v. Allen Christian School, 995 F. Supp. 340, 348 (E.D.N.Y. 1998); see also Dolter v. Wahlert High School, 483 F. Supp. 266 (N.D. Iowa 1980); Vigars v. Valley Christian Center, 805 F. Supp. 802 (N.D. Cal. 1992).

4. E.g., Leslie Griffin, "The Sins of *Hosanna-Tabor*," *Indiana Law Journal* 88 (2013): 981–1020.

5. Transcript of Oral Argument, Hosanna-Tabor Evangelical Lutheran Church and School, http://www.supremecourt.gov/oral_arguments /argument_transcripts/10-553.pdf.

6. Hosanna-Tabor Evangelical Lutheran Church and School v. Equal Em ployment Opportunity Commission, 132 S.Ct. 694 (2012).

7. United States Department of Education, Office for Civil Rights, Dear Colleague Letter: Sexual Violence: Background, Summary, and Fast Facts (April 4, 2011), http://www2.ed.gov/about/offices/list/ocr/docs /dcl-factsheet-201104.html; see also Questions and Answers on Title IX and Sexual Violence (April 2014), http://www2.ed.gov/about/offices /list/ocr/docs/qa-201404-title-ix.pdf.

8. Lynn Langton, Rape And Sexual Assault among College-Age Females, 1995–2013, U.S. Department of Justice Special Report, December 11, 2014, http://www.bjs.gov/content/pub/pdf/rsavcaf9513.pdf; Mark Perry, "Before Declaring That There's a 'Rape Epidemic' in the US, Has Any body Bothered to Check the Actual Data? Apparently Not," *AEI Ideas* (blog), May 17, 2014, http://www.aei-ideas.org/2014/05/before-declar ing-that-theres-a-rape-epidemic-in-the-us-has-anybody-bothered-to

-check-the-actual-data-apparently-not/#mbl; Cathy Young, "The White House Overreaches on Campus Rape," *Minding the Campus* (website), January 23, 2014, http://www.mindingthecampus.com/2014/01/the_white_house_overreaches_on/; White House Council on Women and Girls, Rape and Sexual Assault: A Renewed Call to Action, January 2014, http://www.whitehouse.gov/sites/default/files/docs/sexual_assault_report_1-21-14.pdf.

9. E.g., Gail Schontzler, "Expert Blames Most 'Date Rapes' on Serial Predators," *Bozeman Daily Chronicle*, August 13, 2013, http://www.bozemandailychronicle.com/news/montana_state_university/article_6dfc2c92-03a8-11e3-8f7c-0019bb2963f4.html.

10. Callie Marie Rennison and Lynn A. Addington, "Violence against College Women: A Review to Identify Limitations in Defining the Problem and Inform Future Research," *Trauma, Violence, & Abuse* 15 (2014): 159–69.

11. Quoted in Michelle Goldberg, "Why the Campus Rape Crisis Confounds Colleges," *The Nation*, June 5, 2014, http://www.thenation.com/article/180114/why-campus-rape-crisis-confounds-colleges.

12. United States Department of Education Office for Civil Rights, Questions and Answers on Title IX and Sexual Violence (April 2014), http://www2.ed.gov/about/offices/list/ocr/docs/qa-201404-title-ix.pdf.

13. Ibid., 31.

14. Ibid.

15. Ibid.

16. Joshua Rhett Miller, "Good Grades, Good Home Gets College Student Profiled as Rapist, Claims Lawsuit," *FoxNews.com*, June 6, 2014, http://www.foxnews.com/us/2014/06/05/good-grades-good-home-gets-college-student-profiledas-rapist-claims-lawsuit.

17. KC Johnson, "How Yale Brands Innocent Males as Rapists," *Minding the Campus* (website), August 7, 2014, http://www.mindingthecampus.com/2014/08/how-yale-brands-innocent-males-as-rapists.

18. Ari Cohn, "Swarthmore Admits Treating Student Accused of Sexual Assault Unfairly, Settles Lawsuit," *TheFIRE.org*, November 21, 2014, http://www.thefire.org/swarthmore-admits-treating-student-accused-sexual-assault-unfairly-settles-lawsuit.

19. Wells v. Xavier University, 7 F. Supp. 3d 746 (S.D. Ohio 2014).

20. Goldberg, "Campus Rape Crisis."

21. "Updated: Database of Lawsuits against Colleges and Universities

Alleging Due Process and Other Violations in Adjudicating Sexual Assault," *A Voice for Male Students* (website), November 10, 2014, http://www.avoiceformalestudents.com/list-of-lawsuits-against-colleges-and-universities-alleging-due-process-violations-in-adjudicating-sexual-assault.

22. KC Johnson, "Duke, Grossly Unfair Again, Is Back in Court," *Minding the Campus* (website), May 29, 2014, http://www.mindingthecampus.com/2014/05/duke_grossly_unfair_again_is_b.

23. Hans Bader, "Education Department Illegally Ordered Colleges to Reduce Due-Process Safeguards," *Washington Examiner*, September 21, 2012, http://www.examiner.com/article/education-department-illegally-ordered-colleges-to-reduce-due-process-safeguards.

24. Davis v. Monroe County Board of Education, 526 U.S. 629 (1999).

25. Hans Bader, "No, OCR's April 4, 2011 Dear Colleague Letter Is Not Entitled to Deference," *Washington Examiner*, August 17, 2013, http://www.examiner.com/article/no-ocr-s-april-4-2011-dear-colleague-letter-is-not-entitled-to-deference.

26. E.g., Rattner v. Netburn, 930 F.2d 204 (2d Cir. 1991); Okwedy v. Molinari, 333 F.3d 339 (2d Cir. 2003).

27. Donohue v. Baker, 976 F. Supp. 136 (1997).

28. Dambrot v. Central Michigan University, 55 F.3d 1177 (6th Cir. 1995); UWM Post, Inc. v. Board of Regents of the University of Wisconsin System, 774 F. Supp. 1163 (E.D. Wis. 1991), Doe v. University of Michigan, 721 F. Supp. 852 (E.D. Mich. 1989).

29. For an account of the incident, see Eugene Volokh, "Freedom of Speech in Cyberspace from the Listener's Perspective: Private Speech Restrictions, Libel, State Action, Harassment, and Sex," *University of Chicago Legal Forum* (1996): 377, 419, and n. 148.

30. *Davis*, 526 U.S. 629 (1999).

31. U.S. Department of Education, Office of Civil Rights, First Amendment: Dear Colleague, July 28, 2003, http://www2.ed.gov/about/offices/list/ocr/firstamend.html.

32. Letter from Anurima Bhargava, US Department of Justice Civil Rights Division and Gary Jackson, US Department of Education Office for Civil Rights, to University of Montana President Royce Engstrom, May 9, 2013, http://www.justice.gov/sites/default/files/opa/legacy/2013/05/09/um-ltr-findings.pdf.

33. Federal Government Mandates Unconstitutional Speech Codes at Col-

leges and Universities Nationwide, *TheFIRE.org*, May 17, 2013, http://
www.thefire.org/federal-government-mandates-unconstitutional-
speech-codes-at-colleges-and-universities-nationwide.

34. "'Blueprint' No More? Feds Back Away from New Campus Speech Restrictions," *TheFIRE.org*, November 21, 2013, http://www.thefire.org
/feds-back-away-from-new-campus-speech-restrictions.

35. Will Creeley, "A Year Later, Impact of Feds' 'Blueprint' Comes into Focus," *TheFIRE.org*, August 24, 2014, http://www.thefire.org/year-later-
impact-feds-blueprint-comes-focus.

36. Hans Bader, "Obama Administration Undermines School Safety, Pres-
sures Schools to Adopt Racial Quotas in Student Discipline," *Competitive Enterprise Institute* (blog), January 13, 2014, http://www.open
market.org/2014/01/13/obama-administration-undermines-school
-safety-pressures-schools-to-adopt-racial-quotas-in-student-discipline.

37. Ibid.

38. Ibid.

39. Ibid.

40. Hans Bader, "Minneapolis Adopts Unconstitutional Racial Quotas in
School Discipline," *Competitive Enterprise Institute* (blog), November
12, 2014, https://cei.org/blog/minneapolis-adopts-unconstitutional-ra
cial-quotas-school-discipline.

41. James Bovard, "Perform Criminal Background Checks at Your Peril,"
Wall Street Journal, February 14, 2013, http://online.wsj.com/articles
/SB10001424127887323701904578276491630786614.

Conclusion

1. Bruce Ackerman, "Playing Politics with the Office of Legal Counsel," *Balkinization* (blog), November 24, 2014, http://balkin.blogspot
.com/2014/11/playing-politics-with-office-of-legal.html.

2. Quoted in David Bernstein, "President Obama Should Not Act Unilaterally on Immigration," *Volokh Conspiracy* (blog), November 20, 2014,
http://www.washingtonpost.com/news/volokh-conspiracy/wp/2014
/11/20/president-obama-should-not-act-unilaterally-on-immigration.

3. Immigration Law Professors Letter to President Obama, Execu-
tive Authority to Protect Individuals or Groups from Deportation,
September 4, 2014, http://www.washingtonpost.com/r/2010-2019
/WashingtonPost/2014/09/03/Editorial-Opinion/Graphics/Law%20

Professor%20Letter%20Executive%20Action%20on%20Immigration%20%289.3.14%29%20%28final,%20with%20addresses%29.pdf.

4. E.g., Zachary Price, "Two Cheers for OLC's Opinion," *Balkinization* (blog), November 25, 2014, http://balkin.blogspot.com/2014/11/two-cheers-for-olcs-opinion.html.

5. Michael Dorf, "The Inseparability of Policy Considerations and Resource Considerations in Federal Immigration and Marijuana Enforcement," *Dorf on Law* (blog), November 22, 2014, http://www.dorfonlaw.org/2014/11/the-inseparability-of-policy.html.

6. See Josh Blackman, "Legal Authority for Deferred Deportations of Five Million," *Josh Blackman's Blog*, November 20, 2014, http://joshblackman.com/blog/2014/11/20/the-question-not-answered-by-the-letter-signed-by-100-immigration-law-professors.

7. Neal McCluskey, "Full Facts Needed on the Common Core," *Cato at Liberty*, Cato Institute, January 31, 2014, http://www.cato.org/blog/full-facts-needed-common-core; Neal McCluskey, "Common Core Treats Students Like Soulless Widgets," *U.S. News & World Report*, http://www.usnews.com/debate-club/are-the-common-core-standards-a-good-idea/common-core-treats-students-like-soulless-widgets. States could also gain exemption from NCLB if they got their state university system to certify an alternative curriculum as providing college readiness.

8. Jonathan Chait, "Obama's Immigration Plan Should Scare Liberals, Too," *New York Magazine*, August 11, 2014, http://nymag.com/daily/intelligencer/2014/08/obamas-immigration-plan-should-scare-liberals.html.

INDEX